Historicism

AND

KNOWLEDGE

HISTORICISM

AND

KNOWLEDGE

ROBERT D'AMICO

ROUTLEDGE ■ NEW YORK ■ LONDON

First published in 1989 by

Routledge
an imprint of
Routledge, Chapman & Hall, Inc.
29 West 35th Street
New York, NY 10001

Published in Great Britain by

Routledge
11 Fetter Lane
London EC4P 4EE

Library of Congress Cataloging in Publication Data

D'Amico, Robert.
    Historicism and knowledge / Robert D'Amico
    p. cm.
    1. Knowledge, Theory of—History—20th century. 2. Historicism—
History-20th century. 3 Science—Philosophy—History—20th century.
3. Science—Philosophy—History—20th century. 4. Popper, Karl Raimund,
Sir, 1902– —Contributions in theory of knowledge. I. Title.
BD161.D27   1988   88–20989
149—dc 19
ISBN 0–415–90032–8
ISBN 0–415–90033–6 (pbk)

            British Library Cataloguing in Publication Data
D'Amico, Robert, 1947–
Historicism and knowledge.
1. Philosophy – Critical studies
I. Title
100

ISBN 0–415–90032–8
ISBN 0–415–90033–6 Pbk

Contents

Acknowledgments   vii

Introduction   ix

1   Prophecy   1

2   Situational Logic   20

3   Conceptual Schemes   32

4   Rational Reconstruction   52

5   Historical A Priori   73

6   Objective Knowledge   96

7   Transcendental Turn   119

Conclusion   145

Notes   150

Index   170

Acknowledgments

Between the years 1970 and 1974 I had the rare opportunity to study with three remarkable and vastly different scholars. Sadly, and unexpectedly, the deaths of Marvin Farber, Mitchel Franklin, and Michel Foucault, in the past few years, have made my public appreciation for their direction and support belated. As one acutely aware of this work's shortcomings, I can safely say that it is far better than it would have been because of an opportunity for unimpeded research provided by the National Endowment for the Humanities and a fortunate, if brief, period of study with Ian Hacking who influenced the early stages of this study, unbeknownst to him. I owe a special thanks to David Gross whose very careful reading of a version of this manuscript led to some necessary rewriting. I am especially thankful to the Institute for European and Cultural Studies at the University of Florida that has become my "port in the storm," and especially to Alistair Duckworth, Robert Ray, Greg Ulmer, and Jack Zipes who have been unstinting in their personal and professional support. As a final sad note, our colleague from the Department of Mathematics, Robert Long, was murdered recently in one of those irrational, violent events that continually break the illusion of calm in modern society. He was a partner in many dialogues about this work, and much more, and I felt his absence as I tried to finish this manuscript.

On the personal side, Julie and Christopher sustained me during the past few years by not being crazy and by tolerating my perpetual state of distraction. This work, and a great deal more, would not have been possible but for Susan Armstrong; this one is for you.

Introduction

In a recent article in *The New York Times*[1] music reviewer Donal Henahan recounts an intellectual debate that raged across the pages of the British journal *Music Analysis*. The pretext of the debate between music theorist Allen Forte of Yale University and musicologist Richard Taruskin of University of California at Berkeley, was a technical question. Is Stravinsky's "The Rite of Spring" a tonal or non-tonal piece? What might have appeared to be a simple empirical question became, as Henahan finds surprising, a complex theoretical dispute about such issues as the autonomy of intellectual objects and the methodology of the social sciences.

The two music scholars clashed over whether a musical composition should be studied as a part of some historical and cultural context, in which that piece would be "reconstructed" as the expression of those conditions, or as a specifically musical object, and as such subject only to specifically musical laws and conventions. Forte's method of formal analysis separates the musical object of study from the contingencies of historical context so as to carve out a level of musical abstraction – one concerning physical properties of sound and harmony and conventional laws of music composition. A rigorous musical scholar, like a natural scientist, Forte suggests, ignores cultural and historical variation and concentrates on the formal structure of a musical piece.

Richard Taruskin replies that any attempt to abstract a composition from history, so as to treat only properties of sound and pitch, mistakes musical pieces, which are cultural objects, for natural objects. Taruskin accuses Forte of confusing the "historically situated habits, routines, beliefs, and esthetic assumptions" that make understanding cultural expressions possible with purely physical properties.

In reply to this attack Forte calls Taruskin's view "extreme historicism;" a destructive relativism which reduces the study of music to a futile search for past purposes, motives, intentions and meanings. Taruskin's position would leave musical scholarship with no accessible data and only speculation. If the study of music wants to progress and become scientific it must approach its object with "phenomenological virginity," in Forte's words, making no assumptions beyond what is now present in experience. Forte dismisses as obsolete Taruskin's distinction between natural objects and cultural expressions. Music, like any phenomena, is a natural process and Forte suggests that the social sciences must model the study of culture on the natural sciences. Music may be the easiest case since it responds wholly to natural laws over and above the contingent matter of what a particular society or culture takes as the meaning of that music.

As Henahan suggests, even a "bemused onlooker" suspects that "the disagreement's ramifications extend far beyond the craft of music analysis." And so it does; in fact the debate suggests directly a central issue of philosophy that has haunted modernism since Hegel and is conveyed by the term "historicism." A feature of a good philosophical problem – which of course does not mean a solvable problem – is that it can be generated from the serious intellectual disputes of any discipline. The difficulties Forte and Taruskin have stated so sharply, the nature of objectivity, the distinctiveness of science, and the assumptions needed for inquiry, recall many recent clashes in philosophy and theory of knowledge. Recent trends in literary criticism, historiography, and the continuing debates about the role of classic texts in the educational curriculum may be more familiar examples to the reader than the above dispute about between music theory and musicology.[2]

The following study discusses the position of "historicism," that I consider central to these debates, though often misunderstood. Historicism is a position about the limits of knowledge, how human understanding is always a "captive" of its historical situation. I want to understand why the position has reemerged in modern thought. Is historicism, for example, only the contemporary version of those old sophistic games to deflate and stall any inquiry?[3] Can historicism withstand the variety of rebuttals and dismissals, echoing, for instance, in Forte's response to Taruskin? I am not concerned with the origin or genealogy of the word "historicism," which has already been studied[4], but the status of a philosophical problem which, for better or worse, goes under that name. I have taken the concept as a thread running through what may seem at first a strangely diverse group of philosophers.

The claim that knowledge is historical in this philosophical sense says more than can be satisfied by mere chronology or anecdote. The problem does not concern the obvious fact that all knowledge was produced at some place and time. It is a deeper reflection, or worry to some, that the possibility of objective knowledge is itself "within history." That investigating a world beyond is an elaborate cultural practice.

Historicism, then, is a thesis about limits or boundaries of inquiry and thus part of what could be called "critical theory." Historicism abandons efforts to prove the validity or "rightness" of concepts, rather it treats concepts, standards, and presuppositions as part of historical traditions which constitute objectivity. The question of which concepts are fundamental is always relative to a tradition. For the historicists cultural practices make possible many objective worlds whose internal criteria leave reflection sceptical about the "ultimate" criteria of reference or realism. If theories of knowledge can be said to revolve around the twin themes of "representation" and "expression" historicism holds that knowledge "expresses" a perspective on the world, a context which cannot be transcended. Knowledge only appears to be representative, to picture what is out there. Though such doubts are the stuff of cliched "introduction to philosophy" lectures they have stubbornly survived efforts to treat them as pseudo-problems, as meaningless misuses of language, or idle assaults upon common sense.

Historicism offers a different, albeit sceptical, strategy. Philosophical judgments about knowledge are not to be understood in terms of simple criteria of correctness; rather, historicism pursues a complex reconstruction of the purposes, functions, and contexts of the various intellectual expressions. And philosophical reflection, for the historicists, is no exception to these historical limitations. Consistently, historicism treats its own reflections as bounded by interests, assumptions, and context. Even its own patient reconstructions are provisional claims to be reworked from new perspectives and interests, to be revealed as expressions. According to some, such self-reflection and self-reference leads to a basic incoherence and impossibility. Historicism is making claims about knowledge that it simultaneously shows are not possible.

But at least historicism need not conclude, from its clearly sceptical strategy, that evaluations, universal claims, or standards cannot be formulated. Rather it can take these efforts as constitutive of the world, not representative of the world. For the historicist, philosophical inquiry is neither knowledge of ultimate reality nor common empirical knowledge. But philosophical claims are not thereby nonsense, as positivism argued. In reflecting on what makes knowledge possible philosophical debates are about the deep but alterable constitutive frameworks or "prejudices," as the word was once used without a pejorative connotation, to which objects of knowledge conform. But these arguments can not judge frameworks externally and thus with no single perspective, single description, or single story.

Richard Burian, in an article on history and philosophy of science, a subtheme of my study, claims that the central distinction in modern philosophy of science is between "logicism" and "historicism." As Burian defines historicism; "There are no universally valid methodological and epistemological standards by means of which both science in general and the special sciences may be evaluated."[5] In the spirit of my own effort, Burian shows in the article how the failed attempts at a logical account of science gradually encouraged historicists conclusions.

Historicism is hardly the only modern attitude of scepticism; pragmatism, fallibilism, constructive empiricism, and even deconstruction have rejected traditional philosophical inquiry. What then is considered threatening about historicism? Perhaps in abandoning so completely the distinction between science and ideology, between knowledge and opinion, historicism appears to some as a capitulation to what Plato feared would be the rule of power in knowledge. But historicism does not take arguments from political power or efficiency as any more privileged and beyond question as arguments from essences, nature, or truth itself. There is, I think, a subtle and complex position here which needs a hearing. I have tried to weave the position out of, at first, its best critics. I have not gone on to outline how historicist research into knowledge systems would be done but some hints may be there in the critical debate.

What do philosophers study and what kind of answers can they supply? Philosophers, though not all and not always, study texts and learn how to understand or read them by deepening their understanding of both the context in which the text existed and the reflection possible in the present. Thus they use their historical position in the debate. In other words, philosophers treat the present as historical. As the past is continually read from the interests and tendencies of the present, the past is also used as a way to distance oneself from the present and its assumptions, to reflect upon a tradition by seeing it from another perspective or to enter into another context and thus see it from inside. Historicism provides no answer for what are the correct readings of document and texts, it assumes that there will be and must be indeterminacy. No understanding of the world is a direct and unmediated contact with reality. What we are struggling with in understanding are not the literal words or sentences, nor some simple logical relationships, but the entrenched concepts, presuppositions, and standards which must be teased to the surface and patiently uncovered. Nearly everyone who has struggled with philosophical texts and their notorious ambiguities has had the experience of "breaking through," by suddenly understanding the problem situation of a given text. Who was being disputed, where did the concepts come from, what was the tradition on that issue, what were the reasoning strategies?

Karl Popper was the first to understand historicism as a special philosophical problem. Since I consider his discussion so central to modern philosophy I have discussed his work in some detail in the first two chapters. The study then proceeds to examine various anti-historicist strategies in modern thought, as they grow, explicitly or implicitly out of Popper. My focus is on specific issues such as rational reconstruction, theory of interpretation, relativism, and objective knowledge. In covering these issues I do cross certain boundaries in modern philosophy – for example, moving from the continental tradition as represented by Michel Foucault to the analytic tradition as found in Donald Davidson, Hilary Putnam, and Larry Laudan. My inquiry is guided not by any specific philosophical "style" as much as the versions of these debates that seem to me direct and challenging. As a theme, historicism allows diverse areas and directions of modern philosophy to appear together suddenly and, at least for me, this is often enlightening enough.

1

Prophecy

In 1949 Leo Alexander, a physician, wrote an article "Medical Science Under Dictatorship" which recounts the abuses of medical procedures during the period of German Fascism.[1] Alexander argues that the early, and seemingly innocuous, abolition of controls over euthanasia and abortion created a moral "slippery slope." The readiness of physicians to cooperate or look the other way during the Holocaust had its roots, Alexander argues, in these early decisions of medical convenience. Though the debate about the morality of euthanasia and abortion has continued to rage through the years, along with questions about responsibility for the Holocaust, it is not these arguments but another aspect of Alexander's article that is instructive for the theme of my work.

Alexander speculates that the theoretical and intellectual context which rationalized Fascistic abuses was the "Hegelian doctrine of rational utility." Social planning and the priority of the interests of the society over the individual, he suggests, supplanted traditional moral values and compassion. In Facist Germany, the belief in historical "destiny" combined with historical relativism, Alexander claims, ate away at traditional values and the moral intuitions.

Alexander's claim that Hegel was a utilitarian and a relativist requires a detailed defense. But my particular interest in Alexander's article is not for his philosophical analysis of Hegel. Alexander understood how intellectual debates about the meaning of history could suddenly become critical and decisive for the possibilities of social change.

Alexander's article, like many conservative analyses before and after him, holds that sceptical, relativist, or critical doctrines of philosophy weaken a society's traditions and that specifically the Hegelian doctrine of historicism was responsible for the moral collapse before totalitarianism. Alexander's philosophical reflections were motivated by his personal shock at one of the worst manifestations of the modern age.

It is doubtful that Alexander read, for example, Karl Popper's similar arguments in the early version of *The Poverty of Historicism* that appeared in the journal *Economia* during 1944-1945. Yet, in studies growing from his philosophy of science, Popper came to the same concerns as Alexander over a doctrine Popper named "historicism." Though the word had been used before Popper gave it a precise and polemical meaning and no significant reflection on human knowledge can ignore Popper's detailed criticism and analysis of this doctrine. Popper's reading of Karl Marx, which will begin my discussion, becomes, in my view, the key to Popper's philosophical critique of historicism as a position about knowledge and practice.

In his philosophical work, Popper has sought more than philosophy of science. He has investigated rationality in relation to studies of both society and nature. Popper shares with Marx the view that philosophy and science are not opposed to one another and that philosophy can make progress in the solution of problems once it abandons speculation. Both hold that there are specific social and political implications of otherwise abstract philosophy. Finally Popper's criticism of Marx concerns a "deep" disagreement central to the modern age. Popper did later feel that *The Open Society and Its Enemies*, where he concentrates on the relationship of history and knowledge, was a "detour" in his philosophical career and that the book's notoriety actually deflected attention from his philosophy of science.[2] But the book has emerged as a classic of modern philosophy. Written in an accessible and passionate style Popper's often angry polemic addresses a wide audience with the view that important philosophical problems are, contrary to the fashion of the times, meaningful and resolvable. In this spirit he argues with Marx's historicism as a persuasive and important position requiring a deep theoretical response. What then, according to Popper, was Marx's accomplishment?

In Popper's language Marx "conjectured" that all historical change was determined by the social mode of production, a structure combining the technological forces of production and social relations. From this simple but highly fruitful abstraction Marx outlined a general theory of explanation that dismissed individual or psychological motives, emphasized how action is shaped and constrained by social structure, and reversed the common sense view that societies change solely through their legal, political, or artistic activities. From these general views Marx worked out a periodization of history according to changes in production and a specific analysis of capitalism and its development.

Marx, however, wanted more than a retrospective explanation and sought to predict the direction of history from the nature of the production process. Popper, as will be discussed, considers such "deductions" of class struggle or revolution from his theory a case of Marxist prophecy rather than genuine scientific prediction. But Popper grants that when Marx restricted himself to specific analyses and specifically when he discussed the labor theory of value he produced a genuine scientific "institutional analysis" and a "theoretical success of the first order."[3] Therefore Popper begins by understanding Marx's defense of the labor theory of value before he considers the historicism behind that theoretical approach.

Even though Popper prefers Marx's more technical discussion of the labor theory of value over the broad social analyses for which Marxism is famous, Popper considers the labor theory of value defunct. In fact Popper considers it a contribution to Marx's rehabilitation as a major philosopher to separate his contribution to philosophy of the social sciences from a weak economic theory Marx happened to champion. Even if critics of the labor theory of value are wrong, Popper concedes, it strengthens Marx's overall position to establish "that its [Marxism's] decisive historico-political doctrines can be developed entirely independently of such a controversial theory."[4] In understanding why Popper considers Marx's defense of the labor theory of value redundant and unnecessary, Popper's opposition to historicism emerges.

First of all, to correct a common misunderstanding, I must stress a reason Popper did *not* give for dismissing the theory. Popper did not consider the concept of value a metaphysical and therefore unscientific concept in economic theory. Popper never adhered to the positivist view that theoretical terms should be restricted to reports on observations or only introduced as a short hand for more lengthy lists of observation statements. As long as a theory was testable Popper put no conditions on its basic concepts, their elaboration, or metaphysical commitments.

As Popper was among the first to show, observations are built out of the fabric of theoretical systems.[5] Thus Popper did not see any purpose in opposing concepts because they were not operationally defined or immediately correlated with observations.[6] For Popper science does not require the elimination of all metaphysics, an impossible task anyway, nor is there any way to predict what kind of speculation, since any theoretical orientation goes far beyond sense experience, will generate a good scientific theory. The problem with Marx's treatment of the value theory and its consequent link to historicism lies elsewhere.

The labor theory of value was designed to explain exchange by the measure of labor embodied in a commodity. But the nineteenth century economist David Ricardo, who influenced Marx's formulation of economic theory, had noted an inconvenient circularity in the labor-commanded measure of value when wages were included within the theory.

> If the reward of the labourer were always in proportion to what he produced, the quantity of labor bestowed on a commodity, and the quantity of labor which that quantity would purchase, would be equal, and either might accurately measure the variation of other things: but they are not equal; the first is under many circumstances an invariable standard, indicating correctly the variations of other things; the latter is subject to as many fluctuations as the commodities compared with it.[7]

Thus when the labor theory of value is applied to wages, either the wages are equal exactly to the labor embodied in them or they are not. If the two are equal then wages could act as a standard unlike all other commodities, whose values, according to the theory, fluctuate. But if wages were such a special commodity or measure of exchange the labor theory of value itself would no longer be necessary. However, if wages and the labor embodied in them are unequal and wages fluctuate like other commodities, that condition appears to violate the labor theory of value. Ricardo realized that though he measured the value of a commodity in terms of the quantity of labor in it, a rise or fall in wages did not, as one would conclude, change the value of products.

Marx took over Ricardo's conceptual problem but Marx considered the labor theory of value as a human, conventional arrangement, not a natural necessity. Marx's relationship to the theory was, therefore, ambiguous. Though he defended the theory he considered its categories historical reflections of a society whose economic forces and laws appeared "natural." At the level of appearance, in Marx's view, the categories of classical economics concealed socially created inequalities. While Marx thought that he demonstrated how to salvage the labor theory of value from its internal flaws, his aim was also to demonstrate that modes of exchange were socially constructed arrangements. Marx argued that the labor theory of value, without his critical analysis of its categories, represented social structure as the inevitable result of human psychology or immutable laws of nature. Therefore it was an account of society which denied the possibility of social change and implicitly supported those who benefited from society's inequities.

Marx's contribution, in his own estimation, was the distinction between labor time and labor power. The circularity pointed out by Ricardo occurs because the original theory of value confused, according to Marx, the buying of labor power and the quantity of labor time. What the buyer of the commodity purchases is labor power (that is the commodity bought with wages) and the value of that commodity is measured, like all others, by the quantity of *labor time* necessary to reproduce the laborer. Once that distinction was admitted the feared circularity of the original theory's treatment of wages disappeared. Further Marx thought his distinction showed how the difference between the wages as measured by labor time and the value produced by labor power when utilized in the production process accounted for the excess value (surplus value) that capitalism appropriated as profit.

Popper concedes that the clarification of surplus value was a "clever" accomplishment. But Marx went on to derive certain historical tendencies from the theory. Popper calls Marx's attempted extrapolation a study of the "logic of the [historical] situation." Capitalism intensifies labor productivity so that fewer hours of the working day (labor time) are paid in wages for labor power. The orientation of modern capitalism toward technological change and innovation has, according to Marx, a structural or "institutional explanation." The logic of the situation demands that capitalist production either lengthen the hours worked or produce more for each hour of wage. The more efficient strategy is to get more productivity in each hour of labor power (what Marx calls relative surplus value) and that is done by introducing technology into the labor process. Popper praises these structural historical explanations by Marx because they are examples of how social theory can progress in understanding without appealing to some psychological or philosophical speculations about human nature, as in traditional political philosophy.

In rejecting a purely psychological or ethical account of social forces Marx was defending the autonomy of social science. Popper felt a kinship with Marx's strategies in this case because both thinkers opposed subjectivism in philosophy and social theory. Popper objects to the view that knowledge rests on certain special or privileged psychological acts of belief or perception. Marx also tried to dismiss philosophies which hypothesized a pre-social psychological state of nature, what Marx called, after Defoe's novel *Robinson Crusoe*, the "unimaginative conceits of eighteenth century Robinsonades" about natural life. These approaches had human subjectivity precede the formation of society. In a famous phrase Marx stated that human consciousness does not determine social existence, rather social existence determines consciousness. Popper understands Marx as criticizing the "poverty" of psychologism.

> It must be admitted that the structure of our social environ-
> ment is manmade in a certain sense: that its institutions and
> traditions are the work of neither God nor of nature, but
> the results of human actions and decision, and alterable
> by human actions and decisions. But this does not mean
> that they are all consciously designed, and explicable in
> terms of needs, hopes, or motives. On the contrary, even
> those which arise as the result of conscious and intentional
> human action are, as a rule, *the indirect, the unintended, and
> often the unwanted byproducts of such actions.*"[8]

Though Marx objected to the human costs of capitalist economic development he did not base his criticism on any evil intentions nor did he hope that such abuses would be removed by moral conversion. In rejecting morality Marx was not indulging some dour view of human nature but a non-psychological analysis. As Popper defends it, Marx's structural explanations in history do not rest on the intentions, morals, or plans of any given class and thus are not conspiratorial analyses. On the contrary, Marx hoped to show through his theory why a social class acts as it does, has the values that it does, quite apart from individual motivations and personalities.

In spite of what Popper considers Marx's successful defense of his "viewpoint" on history and society Popper argues at length against Marx's central defense of the labor theory of value. First Popper holds that the labor theory of value is not necessary for the "institutional analysis" of social structure that Marx discovered and practiced. Second, the assumptions necessary to account for exploitation within capitalism render the labor theory of value redundant. Finally Marx's real reasons for defending the labor theory of value are his acceptance of essentialist and historicist doctrines, which Marx mistakenly took as a guarantee of the scientific status of his work.

I consider the third point the most important of these three arguments as it concerns what Popper considers Marx's fatal commitment to the "deep" historicist worldview. In the first two objections Popper argues that since one buys or sells as cheaply or dearly as possible, the labor-commanded measure of value is irrelevant and unnecessary. Selling above the "value" of the commodity, or buying below it, is merely an indirect, convoluted way of talking about how the market regulates exchange. What the term "value" tries to express and substantialize is simply the long term stability of "prices" as dictated by market mechanisms. Popper concludes that since the participants in economic exchange do not *perceive* the value component (they only perceive prices) and since the oscillations that value is supposed to regulate can be explained more efficently with only prices and a simple law of supply and demand the complexity of the concept of value can be avoided. For Popper then "the laws of supply and demand are not only necessary but also sufficient to explain all the phenomena of 'exploitation' which Marx observed –
. . . Thus the value theory turns out to be a completely redundant part of Marx's theory of exploitation; and this holds independently

of the question of whether the value theory is true."[9]

In this passage Popper raises a serious and complex set of philosophical questions about what constitutes a "good" theory. He seems to argue that whether a theory is true or not is less important than its explanatory efficiency which can be measured by the simplicity of "fit" between the theory and the observed frequencies. Thus what Popper means by "redundant" in this case is that the complications of the value theory should be replaced by a simpler account. The approach Popper defends then is that a theory is a "tool" for measuring or predicting phenomena and our goal should be a useful and efficient tool since we can never know which account is true. Of course Marx did not take such an instrumental view of his task and in fact thought that success in the prediction of prices, for example, may have nothing to do with representing "what is really the case." Marx, to use modern terminology, was a realist about philosophy of science. Therefore he could hardly have been persuaded by Popper's appeal to the admitted simplicity of "laws" of supply and demand which Marx considered "superficial" economics. For Marx the labor theory of value represented the historical force that shaped society, namely human labor power, and thus was not redundant when compared with other, albeit equivalently useful economic theories.

In his later writings Popper concedes that his early works were unclear about the issue of scientific realism.[10] The position of his first published work in philosophy, *The Logic of Scientific Discovery*, which predates *The Open Society*, suggests that the scientific methodological criteria and the refutation of theories by crucial experiments are conventions or rules adopted by the scientific community.[11] In other words Popper does not adhere to the view that the best theory is the one that represents what the world is really like. Popper was an anti-empiricist and thus shares that with the modern meaning of realism. But he began as a radical sceptic about the certainty or representational status of knowledge. If Popper was still a conventionalist and anti-realist when he wrote on the social sciences his appeal to simplicity against Marx is understandable. I am convinced, however, that Popper falls back on arguments from simplicity and methodological convention in his stand against Marx's theoretical qualifications because he is already convinced of the falsity of the historicist doctrine quite apart from problems of historical explanation and evidence. In other words, the fundamental issue in the study of history for Popper is not methodological but metaphysical.

What is interesting about this precise issue is that Marx's distinction between prices and values, which Popper is opposing, was in part the expression of Marx's realism about philosophy of science. Marx had not considered success in the prediction of prices as an aim of his theory, just as he was not bothered by the non-empirical status of the term value. In fact Marx accuses political economy of confusing "laws" with inductive regularities and real forces with what merely "appears."

> Classical political economy borrowed from every-day life the category "price of labor" without further criticism, and then simply asked the question, how is the price determined? . . . If demand and supply balance, the oscillation of prices ceases, all other conditions remaining the same. But then demand and supply also *cease to explain anything* [emphasis added]. The price of labor, at the moment when demand and supply are in equilibrium, is . . . determined independently of the relation of demand and supply. It was therefore found that the natural price was the object that actually had to be analyzed.[12]

Marx argued that science should criticize experience and that the mere identification of regularities was not explanation. Here Marx sounds like Popper's own later defense of what he calls metaphysical realism. At any rate, Popper's effort to refute the labor theory of value on purely theoretical or a priori grounds ends up treating "supply and demand" as a simple, unquestioned fact of experience. But in this way Popper, even against his own philosophical attitude, suppresses the theory-ladenness of any such interpretation and construction from possible experience. Marx's anti-empiricism made him justifiably suspicious of appeals to utility and simplicity in explanation. Marx approached any appeal to "common opinion," given his theory of ideology, as the beginning of critique rather than the termination of debate. He criticized political economy for "worshipping appearances" or failing to grasp that "the form of appearance . . . makes the actual relation invisible and indeed presents to the eye the precise opposite of that relation."[13]

The apparent oscillation of prices and supply and demand conceals a real theoretical dispute.

For example, John Weeks's *Capital and Exploitation* which holds that, "Perception plays no role in the determination of exchange rates," considers the distinguishing feature of Marxism to be that the mode of production determines exchange and supply and demand, even though it appears reversed.[14] If Weeks's argument is defensible Popper is wrong to assume that the law of supply and demand is theoretically equivalent to Marx's use of the labor theory of value. Of course, supply and demand will "work" within normal conditions to allow for predictions of prices. But these apparent regularities are the result, not the cause, Weeks argues, of how production is organized.

In making his point Weeks suggests a thought experiment involving a subsistence agricultural society in which only the final products are sold and in which all the other aspects of the production process are either naturally present or made by the agricultural unit itself. In such a situation prices, if needed, would be determined by competition between units to sell excess goods. A simplifying assumption is that there is no other exchange than the final goods since all materials needed to produce are part of the respective unit.

In this imaginary situation the more efficient farmers will realize a higher return for their goods in the market. But the example is designed to show that the "law" of the market is not sufficient to explain this situation. The balance of supply and demand is not an explanatory device but the very situation to be explained.

In this thought example the crucial differences in success are immutable (i.e., family size, fertility of the soil). Since the units are self-sufficient, failure to profit in the market involves only failure to sell the excess of the produced utilities. Thus the example artificially highlights that while supply and demand regulate the exchange of these excess use values what makes that regularity work is the kind of production or labor involved in the process.

In continuing the analogy we can ask what would change the imaginary "feudal" units? Clearly if products *had* to be bought and sold and there was distinct labor for maintenance of the unit and labor for exchange in the market, the entire effect of the market would change. Suddenly the forces of supply and demand would be "internalized" by the unit and these new effects of supply and demand would result from the separation of production for exchange from production for use. The result would be a version of Marx's distinction between prices and values. This imaginary and simplistic example does not prove that the labor theory of value is correct. It only shows that, even if questionable, it is not simply redundant, as Popper argues, with regard to supply and demand or prices. It is Popper's assumption that values and prices are the same that makes the labor theory of value redundant. But that assumption begs the central question. Thus Popper's first two arguments against Marx's theoretical approach fail in demonstrating that Marx's theory is unnecessarily complicated. The argument rests on a defense of simplicity or instrumentalism in judging theories inconsistent with both Marx's views and Popper's own later defense of realism.

Popper's third criticism about essentialism, however, is more important and leads directly to his argument against historicism. Popper holds that essentialism and historicism are related positions because "these far-reaching historicist consequences . . . were slumbering for more than twenty centuries, 'hidden and undeveloped' in Aristotle's essentialism."[15] Therefore Marx's effort to rescue the labor theory of value and understand history as the unfolding of human productive power is actually the expression of an essentialist conception of humanity with the historicist belief in patterns, laws, and prediction in social and cultural history.

From the beginning of his work in philosophy of science Popper did not consider attacks on metaphysics as worthwhile. He was more concerned with eliminating what he calls "pseudo-science," and did not consider it advisable or possible to eliminate metaphysical speculation. Popper was especially critical of the positivist theory that metaphysical statements are meaningless. Popper simply argues that the verification theory of meaning is hopelessly narrow and seeks, mistakenly, a single criterion of meaning. Metaphysical doctrines are, in Popper's view, both meaningful and the source of important science. Therefore his opposition to historicism and essentialism is not simply that they are speculations. Even speculations can be judged, Popper holds, through what he calls "critical rationalism." Though we can never prove the truth of the fundamental concepts of understanding we can reason about and challenge their implications. Essentialism, then, from the viewpoint of critical rationalism, is an assumption that all theories should strive to describe the "essential natures of things" and in doing so these theories are neither in need nor susceptible of further explanation: they are ultimate explanations and to find them is the ultimate aim of the scientist. This . . . doctrine is the one I have called essentialism."[16]

Popper opposes this assumption because in his view it weakens the role of criticism of theories and, though the conjecture that nature hides from observation may be fruitful, the aim of ultimate explanations asserts dogmatic and unattainable standards for scientific progress.

> In other words my criticism tries to show that whether essences exist or not the *belief does not help us in any way* [emphasis added] and indeed is likely to hamper us: so that there is no reason why scientists should assume their existence.[17]

Once again, Popper appears to invoke an instrumental argument in which the truth or falsity of essences as objects in reality is treated as less important than whether belief in these realities makes the job of theoretical explanation more cumbersome or difficult. Thus Marx's case for the labor theory of value, no matter how good the argument, is fatally flawed because it is sustained by a belief that there is an ultimate explanation of historical events.

One problem with this point is that though Marx does use the Aristotelian vocabulary of "human essence" it is not clear that he also thought, as Popper holds, that the labor theory of value is an ultimate explanation.[18] Marx defends the labor theory of value as the best theory available, yet he also criticized interpretations of it as a natural law or the expression of inexorable and inevitable forces. In his criticisms of classical political economists Marx was explicitly anti-essentialist in that he treats all theoretical categories, including his own, as historical. Marx does appear to have made a metaphysical commitment to materialism and realism, but, as Popper's himself shows, a realist is not the same as an essentialist.

Clearly the argument most often attributed to Popper concerning Marx is the position that a theory which cannot be tested or fails to accept its refutation or falsification by counterevidence is pseudo-scientific. But careful readers of Popper have always known that he does not argue in this fashion against Marx. Marx's theory is scientific because it is testable. In being refuted it joins the long list of scientific learning through trial and error. Thus the case of Marx is to be distinguished from a pseudo-scientific theory which through ad hoc modification or inherent concepts cannot be tested at all.

Surprisingly, Popper's famous doctrine of falsification plays a rather minor role in *The Open Society*, even though a popularized account of these arguments in the 1953 essay "Science: Conjectures and Refutations" makes "testability" the sole issue. In the 1953 essay, however, Popper had a quite different context and aim. His point was no longer, as in *The Open Society*, to criticize the foundations of contemporary social science and the threat of historicism but to demonstrate that the positivist theory of science, namely testing for confirmation and corroboration, is worthless. It must admit as scientific such theories as astrology, psychoanalysis, and Marxism, because all of them have overwhelming confirmatory evidence. Popper holds, therefore, that the positivist doctrine of verification by inductive evidence leads counter-intuitively to a very "loose" definition of science.

Historically some members of the Vienna Circle, against whom Popper struggled theoretically from his very first works, were committed to precisely these doctrines and accepted positivism because it lent support to their socialist politics. Popper may have had actual disagreements in mind when he wrote both *The Open Society* and the later essay in *Conjectures and Refutations*. However, by 1953, it should be noted, positivism was neither committed to nor identified with either Marxism or psychoanalysis.[19]

In the 1953 essay, Popper's point is that while Marx's theory generated research it protected its historicist bias against disproof. While Popper stresses that we learn from such failures, in fact we learn exclusively from failed attempts, keeping a theory alive through ad hoc support and spurious modification is a sign that some deeper, unquestioned, and perhaps unconscious commitment overrides critical reasoning. In *The Open Society* Popper says, "Marx was wrong when he prophesized that the conditions which he observed were to be permanent if not changed by revolution and even more when he prophesized that they would get worse. *The facts have refuted these prophesizes* [emphasis added]."[20]

In 1953 Popper distinguishes between Marx and his followers.

> [Marx's] predictions were testable and in fact falsified. Yet instead of accepting the refutations the followers of Marx re-interpreted both the theory and evidence in order to make them agree. In this way they rescued the theory from refutation, but they did so at the price of adopting a device which made it irrefutable . . . by this stratagem they destroyed its much advertised claim to scientific status.[21]

In *The Open Society* Popper considers in detail two related predictions that follow from Marx's treatment of the labor theory of value. First is Marx's prediction of a falling rate of profit and second is the immiseration of the working class through capitalist appropriation.

Marx thought the labor theory of value revealed contradictions inherent in the capitalist mode of production. These contradictions or tensions were the result of purely economic decisions. In using the term contradiction Marx did not mean a literal logical incoherence within the theory. Rather he detects incompatible or counteracting strategies within social institutions, practical actions, and shows how these problems are concealed or obscured by theoretical categories. Marx's point would be similar to a demonstration that because a bureaucracy may demand both accountability and secrecy, its actions have an internal inconsistency or tension which often leads to what Popper calls the study of "unforeseen consequences." Of course often there is more precision about the fact of the conflict than the specific consequences. In Marx's approach the capitalist, in the very exigencies that demand lowering the wage rate for his workers, unintentionally lowers the profit rate. This practical dilemma is understood, according to Marx, by stressing the distinction between labor intensive and capital intensive industries. Marx used this difference as a key to an "institutional logic" linking together economic strategies and technological innovation.

Marx divided the capital in an industry between the value of the machinery of production, which he called constant capital, and the value of the labor which he called variable capital. The ratio between these two types of capital in any industry is called by Marx the "organic composition of capital." A high organic composition means an industry which is highly technologized and thus the amount of constant capital is greater than variable capital. Marx concluded that as capitalism matured industries which accumulated investments in technology, and thus higher rates of relative surplus value, would effectively monopolize against competition and market mechanisms. Either of these tendencies makes the labor theory of value inapplicable.

But still assuming the competitive conditions for the value theory Marx does predict that a technological innovation in production will only initially raise the rate of profit, or what Marx calls surplus value. Machinery simply raises the productivity of each hour of labour. Why, according to Marx, is this advantage only temporary?

Marx explains that the labor needed to produce a product is a socially determined measure. It is the labor "socially necessary" to produce something. In other words, to forestall an often repeated objection to the labor theory of value, a pair of shoes made by myself, probably taking hundreds of hours, would not thereby be worth more than a pair made by a machine (or a skilled shoemaker) in a fraction of the time. Marx's clarification may at first seem a mere "dodge" to avoid a theoretical problem, but is, in fact, central.

Marx built his theoretical picture of the historical formation of economies on the ability of capitalism to generate increased rates of production due to competition. But he also argued that capitalist revolutions are unending since the technological advances rapidly become obsolete. The new more efficient labor time simply becomes the "socially necessary" time and all competition must adjust, at least under ideal conditions, to the new minimum. With the socially necessary labor time at the new limit all the excess created by the innovation evaporates so as to require new innovations and a new cycle, on and on into the future.

Though Marx's use of the term "contradiction" with regard to social theory bothers many critics, Popper offers a useful clarification when he described Marx as producing an institutional analysis or a "logic of the [historical] situation." The term contradiction means that actions have unintended consequences. Given a certain social structure of production and exchange the motives and intentions of agents may be quite different from the "unforeseen" consequences.

With this very brief review of its theoretical context we can now reexamine Marx's prediction that the rate of profit will fall. Actually the prediction is more like a necessary condition of Marx's basic concepts. Marx's often disputed conclusion depends on a crucial assumption that the mass of excess or surplus value produced must fall if fewer workers and thus labor power are employed producing value. Where the conditions are capital intensive, that is for Marx a higher ratio of constant capital to variable capital, there will be the advantage of less wages but there must be, correspondingly, less value available.

> [A] portion of capital, which was previously variable, i.e. had been turned into living labour, had been turned into machinery, i.e. constant capital which does not produce surplus value. It is impossible for instance to squeeze as much surplus value out of two as out of 24 workers.[22]

Marx's argument, which is simply a restatement of the labor theory of value, could then be described as a version of the second law of thermodynamics. The rate of surplus value cannot rise at the same time that the labor power in the factory declines. Machinery, like any commodity in the labor theory of value, is worth as much labor as embodied in it and therefore cannot generate more value than its worth. If it did it would be worth more and if it did that consistently the second law would be violated. The source of any surplus must be added labor power, that is Marx's fundamental precondition. Marx then simply extrapolated that as the amount of labor power utilized fell, the value of products and, in the long run, the rate of profit must also fall. These two incompatible results, lowering wages through increased technical production and falling rates of profit, were the unintended and unwanted consequences of "rational" economic decisions. Human action was "caught" and understanding these limits allowed for a structural explanation of the conditions that made a given historical action possible.

Popper considers this argument ingenious and fruitful. But Popper also concludes that these theoretical predictions were falsified by subsequent events which thereby refuted the whole theory. Marx's genuine contribution was an institutional analysis and what Popper calls a "general interpretation" in history which gives examples of prototype explanations. But in quite correctly trying to make predictions, since that means the theory is testable, Marx was led to conclude, in Popper's words, that "the intensity of the worker's suffering" would increase. Popper simply replies that "if we look at actual developments . . . there is no doubt that the worker's suffering was considerably worse in Marx's day."[23]

The phrase "if we look at actual developments" is where Popper introduces the evidence going against or falsifying Marx's prediction. Popper does not consider what theoretical perspective generated the counterevidence, rather he treats it as a manifest fact of observation. Popper explicitly disallows any attempt to qualify Marx's prediction by, for example, considering such possible countermeasures as state intervention into the economy. Nor does Popper want to allow any challenge of counterevidence as merely "apparent," as the ideological semblance of reality.[24] Marx's theory of ideology would then be used as an automatic device for fending off contrary analyses. In Popper's account then any successful economic reform, or what he calls "counter cycle policy," would, by definition, refute Marx's predictions.

In general Popper uses the criteria of falsification much more rigidly and crudely in discussing the social sciences than when discussing physics and the natural sciences.[25] Thus some of the weaknesses of falsification as a strategy for science and rational decisions appear more obvious in these discussions than in Popper's philosophy of the natural sciences. Specifically Popper often treats the falsifying evidence as non-controversial and non-defeasible when he dismisses continued research within certain theoretical frameworks such as Marxism. He does not allow the disputed theory to challenge the counterevidence, modify its predictions, or qualify its concepts. Popper wants to show definitively that historicism is a *special* metaphysical obstacle or prejudice within the social sciences in general.

> But a close view of Marx's successes shows that *it was nowhere his historicist method which led him to success, but always the methods of institutional analysis*. . . . Nowhere in these analyses do the typical historicist "laws of development," or stages, or periods, or tendencies play any part whatsoever. On the other hand, none of Marx's more ambitious historicist conclusions, none of his "inexorable laws of development" and his "stages of history which cannot be leaped over," has ever turned out to be a successful prediction. Marx was successful *only* in so far as he was analyzing institutions and their functions.[26]

Imre Lakatos calls Popper's early "loose" formulation of his doctrine "naive falsification." By "naive" Lakatos means that Popper equates a refuting instance with a "natural" or common sense, manifest observation whose single occurrence is sufficient to abandon a whole theory. As Lakatos puts it: "For the naive falsificationist a theory is *falsified* by a ('fortified') 'observational' statement which conflicts with it (or which he decides to interpret as conflicting with it)."[27] Hilary Putnam also argues against Popper that "some scientific theories cannot be overthrown by experiments and observations *alone*, but only by alternative theories."[28] Putnam points out that since refuting evidence must have a theoretical context (on Popper's own account) and since that theoretical context influences perception, these conditions leave falsifying evidence and the falsificationist strategy of research a matter of conventional agreement – always open to challenge.

In *Conjectures and Refutations* Popper does grant that observations are always "indirect" and theoretical. I am not holding that these admissions exclude the use of falsification entirely. Refutation is a genuine aspect of research and its clarification by Popper is important. But the strategy requires some conventional agreement especially if it is going to be dramatically applied as a method to exclude certain theoretical assumptions or research programs. However, in Popper's account of Marx the conterevidence is in the form of "common opinion" or direct observation as in the phrase "if we look at actual developments." But the Popper who defines philosophy as "critical analysis of the appeal to the authority of 'experience'" cannot also take certain "facts," "evidence," or "well known cases" as magically abstracted from theoretical contexts and debate, standing beyond question.[29]

Popper remains convinced, however, that Marxists (if not Marx himself) increased the ad hoc character of Marx's theory of history, making it "messier" in an effort to escape the cruel judgment of historical experience. Popper also thinks that Marx opened the door to such abuse in qualifying his predictions as "tendencies" all due to the deep and unquestioned historicist conception of objectified historical laws.[30]

Popper's examples of faulty ad hoc strategies are in the work of Engels and Lenin who suggested that perhaps imperialism, a condition Marx explicitly excluded from his study of capital, might account for the historical discrepancies in the theory. Engels, for instance, thought that the worker's considerable improvement in the later part of the nineteenth century in England was due to Britain "exploiting the whole world." Lenin then extended this argument in a famous essay that pictured the industrial working class within an imperialist country as becoming more "bourgeois" due to increased wages made possible by colonial markets, raw materials, and colonial monopolies. Popper's reply to these reconstructions is; "I do not believe that the auxiliary hypothesis whose history I have sketched can save the law of increasing misery; for this hypothesis is itself refuted by experience."[31]

Popper gave, in his view, a direct and simple refutation of Marxism. But the falsification of Marx's predictions is finally not the central issue for Popper. Marx had developed, under the influence of Hegel, an historicist approach to reason and theory of knowledge – a metaphysics that underlay what Popper sees as theoretical abuse and which, unfortunately in his opinion, profoundly marked modern thought. It is this philosophy of historical reason that is at the root of Popper's concern; a metaphysical assumption that historical experience is only possible because "history has a meaning."

2

Situational Logic

I have examined what Popper called the "unconscious" relationship between theory of knowledge and a view of history and politics. This concern, along with his interest in science, led him to formulate a broad philosophical understanding of reason and the role of hypotheses and criticism. Now I turn more specifically to the metaphysical viewpoints about history that Popper rejects. In spite of his avowed position, specifically his position against relativism, I consider Popper's philosophy of history a motivation for the rise of historicism in recent philosophy. I will argue that Popper's refutation of historicism was actually a refutation of realism in the social sciences and specifically a realist account of historical explanation. In an effort, however, to salvage the idea of the social sciences Popper developed what he called a "logic of the situation" or "zero model of rational construction" which emphasized instrumental or conventional standards of historical reconstruction and the importance of the distinction between reasons and causes. These themes led, contrary to Popper's intention, to revived interest in historicist epistemology. Thus Popper's views encouraged and provided the motivation for positions about the history of knowledge and science that he would later dismiss as relativist and sceptical. His original arguments against historicism led then to an account of historical reconstruction.

There are two senses of the term historicism that must be distinguished in Popper's discussion and within the tradition he is analyzing. First there is the conception that Popper defines and then rejects. History obeys a lawful order or logic and knowing its "laws of emergence" allows for historical predictions. The second conception of historicism is found, I argue, not only in a tradition prior to Popper but in Popper's own situational logic. In this second sense historicism emphasizes that ways of reasoning are entrenched or embedded in contexts that can be judged either internally or retrospectively from the present. Rationality is inseparable from and judged internally to changing problem situations. There is no automatic rationality and thus no single, correct account. Historical interpretations can be judged in terms of their practicality, utility, simplicity, or theoretical fertility, but not as representations of reality.[1] Historicism, in this second sense, investigates how different frameworks make historical understanding possible, and rejects efforts to determine which of these frameworks is true.

Popper readily admits that he coined the first sense of historicism as a new usage of the term and prides himself on that since he wants to dismiss quibbles over theoretical terminology. Popper argues that philosophy is concerned with problems, not word use, and whatever term grasps the problem situation is finally unimportant. Thus rather than an actual position Popper invents a thought experiment or "ideal type."

> I have tried to perfect a theory which has often been put forward, but perhaps never in a fully developed form. This is why I have deliberately chosen the somewhat unfamiliar label "historicism." By introducing it I hope I shall avoid merely verbal quibbles; for nobody, I hope, will be tempted to question whether any of the arguments here discussed really or properly or essentially belong to historicism, or what the word historicism really or properly or essentially means.[2]

I doubt that there has ever been a more forlorn hope – even though Popper may have been facetious in hoping that his opponents, whom he characterizes as essentialists, would not resort to an essentialist defense of their views. Thus I have suggested there are two "problem situations" captured by the term historicism and my argument is that Popper's refutation of the first problem, namely the possibility of historical predictions and laws, actually led to the emergence within his philosophy of the second problem, namely the historicity of understanding through reconstructions.

Why is *The Poverty of Historicism* such a perplexing book and one which has elicited such a confused debate? Popper attributes this confusion to the way the book was written. He wrote it as a lecture which gradually began to expand and whose section on essentialism grew into *The Open Society*.[3] I believe there is more here than poor organization and a messy style.

The book's initial confusion occurs because Popper's stand on the distinction or similarity between the natural and social sciences is ambiguous. Popper attacks both naturalistic and non-naturalistic historicism. The naturalistic brand of historicism seeks a unification of the natural and social sciences by accepting natural laws in history, whereas the non-naturalistic brand treats social, historical laws as autonomous and irreducible to natural laws. Because, according to Popper's usage, historicism seeks laws of history his refutation simply concentrates on how the very idea of law or prediction in history is impossible, without also deciding whether such laws are natural or social. He does say, at first, that he agrees with the view that there is a common method in the natural and social sciences.[4] But, as I will show, Popper's defense of what he calls the "zero degree method" of historical construction demands, on the contrary, the distinction between the social and natural sciences. Thus a fundamental confusion was bound to arise for those who held that historicism, which traditionally separated the social and natural sciences, did so precisely *because* there could not be historical laws.

Readers such as Herbert Marcuse or Calvin Rand began with the assumption that historicism was not, as Popper said, "an unfamiliar label" but the name of a familiar position about how cultures influence knowledge. Rand says:

> Hence the historicist . . . is directed to look upon each person, event, nation or era as a unique individual, which develops over a period of time through its own internal means. . . . Putting it in another way, the historian notices that each individual is rooted in its own time and place in the course of history and that it grows out of the specific circumstances of the times.[5]

These authors took Popper's arguments against there being historical laws as tantamount to a *defense of historicism*. To add fuel to this reading Popper, later in his book, substitutes for historical laws what he calls "general interpretations" in history, the aim of *understanding* historical problem situations. Thus Popper's concluding position – which Popper presents is an alternative to historicism – resembles the position traditionally intended by the term. Popper even describes himself in later writings as contributing to "the theory of understanding ('hermeneutics') which has been much discussed by students of the humanities."[6]

The beginning of *The Poverty of Historicism* reveals, keeping the above ambiguity in mind, what Popper takes as the common assumption between naturalist and anti-naturalist historicism.

> I mean by historicism an approach to the social sciences which assumes that *historical prediction* is their principal aim, and which assumes that this aim is attainable by discovering the "rhythms" or "patterns," the "laws" or the "trends" that underlie the evolution of history.[7]

In historicist prediction, Popper argues, the difference between social and natural laws is unimportant.[8] Popper thus begins by excluding a possible position which would seek historical understanding *and* forego the search for either natural or sociological laws.[9] But such a position emerges by the end of the book as Popper's own view of historical explanation. Situational analysis aims at historical understanding (rather than prediction) and pluralism in historical reconstruction (rather than historical laws). Popper's philosophy of history shares with the second sense of historicism its traditional opposition to historical realism or naturalism. In fact what Popper considers his definitive argument against historicism in *The Poverty of Historicism* actually deals with the failure of realist and naturalist models of explanation to apply to history.

Popper obscures his similarity with an historicist approach to knowledge because the protean shapes of his term "historicism" allow him, at selected moments, to collapse the quest for historical laws *and* relativism under the same term historicism, and a single theoretical refutation. For example, he argues that historicists emphasize the role of interests and "prejudices" in the formation of knowledge. From such a notion of perspective, traditional objectivity as achieved in the natural sciences is unattainable. There are, as Popper agrees, "as many tendencies in the social sciences as can be found in social life; as many standpoints as there are interests." Thus Popper concludes that historicism leads to a relativism in which "objectivity, and the ideal of truth, are altogether inapplicable in the social sciences *where only success – political success – can be decisive*" [emphasis added].[10]

Relativism is another historicist sin. But Popper fails to come back to this passage and explain how his position about reconstruction differs from this similar argument for the relativism of knowledge as due to human interest. Popper, in fact, defends pluralism in reconstructions, the role of interests in knowledge, and a limited "perspectival" objectivity in the study of history.[11] Historical interpretation seeks, as he says, to "reconstruct the *problem situation* in which the acting person finds himself, and to show how and why his action constituted a solution of this problem."[12] He is thus led in *The Open Society* to conclude; "For since each generation has its own troubles and problems, and *therefore its own interests and its own point of view*, [emphasis added] it follows that each generation has a right to look upon and re-interpret history in its own way, which is complementary to that of previous generations."[13]

When Popper attacks the relativist side of historicism he argues that the position makes practical success rather than objectivity decisive for the social sciences. This reply implies that Popper's reason for rejecting historicism is his general opposition to making judgments on alternative theories on instrumental grounds. But when Popper explains and defends what he calls a "logic of the situations" and rational reconstruction he emphasizes that he makes no realist assumptions about such explanations. In fact to believe that historical explanations describe real forces and causes is historicist. Popper allows only "sweep" and "fertility," i.e., instrumental criteria, to count in the weighing of alternative historical accounts. He claims: "There is necessarily a plurality of interpretations which are fundamentally on the same level of both, suggestiveness and arbitrariness (even though some of them may be distinguished by their *fertility* – a point of some importance)."[14] Popper thus accepts and recommends the weak objectivity he isolates earlier as a "poverty" of historicism. Popper's account of interpretation by interests or context in the logic of the situation is simply relativist. I have already discussed how in *The Open Society* Popper rejects Marx's labor theory of value on instrumental grounds.[15] As I discussed, Popper concludes that the concept of value is unnecessary to historical explanations whether or not the value theory of economics is true.[16] Is the problem with historicism, therefore, its realist or its relativist implications?

In parts of *The Poverty of Historicism* Popper holds that both historical theories and natural scientific theories are "general interpretations." Then the argument is made that historical understanding, through multiple perspectives, can only produce accounts that are more or less "sweeping." The mistake comes in taking such "general interpretations" of history as representative of real causes and forces and thus something like historical laws. Historicism is a fallacy of objectivism. But, as Popper proclaims, "history does not have a meaning."

Popper always objects to a belief in "ultimate explanations" and I might be accused of confusing his position against certainty with reviving "historicist scepticism." But while Popper claims that all knowledge is fallible, he also considers that position consistent with definitive standards of whether or not a theory is scientific and whether or not a position is rational. Fallibilism shows that dogmatism or certainty about knowledge is irrational, but does not lead to total or self-defeating scepticism because of the ability to disprove theories by logical refutation. But when Popper argues for these conclusions concerning historical interpretations the emphasis is entirely on the side of the sceptical and fallible (and thus objectivist historicism is seen as dangerously dogmatic). When Popper discusses the natural sciences the emphasis shifts to a minimal guarantee that the logic of testing determines which hypotheses are scientific and which responses to counterevidence are legitimate.

In his later writings Popper came out strongly against instrumentalism, especially within physics where he feared it made the refutation of theories impossible. However Popper's scepticism never fully disappears. It reemerges whenever he confronts the quest for certainty, as in essentialism, or any claim that our knowledge *represents* reality.[17] Popper's disagreement with essentialism is thus quite metaphysical. Essentialists deny reality "to all that is colorful, varied, individual, indeterminate or indescribable in our world," but Popper does not concern himself with arguments for the existence or non-existence of essences.[18]

> In other words my criticism tries to show that *whether*
> *essences exist or not the belief does not help us in any way*
> *and indeed is likely to hamper us* [emphasis added]: so that
> there is no reason why scientists should assume their
> existence.[19]

Popper's grounds for rejecting Marx's theory of value, for instance, is not based on some definitive standards of rationality or science but on historical grounds. That is, Marx's theory is judged as a social theory or general interpretation of history, which responds to the problem situation *which the theorist faced*. Marx's approach to history is neither true nor false but makes possible a fertile or sweeping interpretation. Realism in the social sciences would mean that Marxism discovered the single historical plot, trend, or direction. In such assertions about trends or laws, Popper's own definition of historicism, the contrary evils of dogmatism and relativism lurk. Popper's logic of the situation combats belief in historical forces and laws by restricting interpretation to the weaker condition of responding to "human interests." Any stronger claim to certainty, Popper warns, leads to totalitarianism. My point is that Popper's antidote to ·"hysterical historicism" is indistinguishable from the sceptical, second sense of historicism, outlined above.

> To sum up, there can be no history of "the past as it
> actually did happen"; there can only be historical interpre-
> tations, and none of them final; and every generation has a
> right to frame its own. . . . But am I justified in refusing to
> the historicist the right to interpret history in his own
> way? . . . My answer to this question is that historicist
> interpretations are of a peculiar kind. . . . .the historicist
> does not recognize that *it is we who select and order the facts*
> *of history* [emphasis added], but he believes that "history
> itself," or the "history of mankind," determines, by its
> inherent laws, ourselves, our problems, our future, and
> even our point of view.[20]

In *The Open Society* Popper offered a combination of moral, political, and ideological arguments against historicism. In the compressed presentation of *The Poverty of Historicism* Popper makes a conceptual or *a priori* argument against historical laws per se.

Aside from a myriad of digressions Popper's central argument against laws of history rests on correcting a misinterpretation of laws and prediction in philosophy of science. What Popper calls an inductive view of science holds that knowledge proceeds by generalization from collected evidence. In this view a law is the result of such generalization and can be verified by an inductive procedure. But Popper repeats that he has advocated an "interpretation of scientific method as deductive, hypothetical, selective by way of falsification, etc."[21]

Thus in Popper's conjectural method laws are not descriptions of forces, but highly improbable and general "guesses" about nature. Further, no law can be proven by its predictive success. Predictions are artificial and constrained experimental situations neither foretelling the future nor proving the truth of the theory being tested. The purpose of a prediction is only the logical possibility of refutation.

> [N]atural laws . . . can never do more than *exclude certain possibilities*. . . . In general it is only by the use of artificial experimental isolation that we can predict physical events . . . We are very far from being able to predict, even in physics, the precise results of a concrete situation, such as a thunderstorm, or a fire.[22]

Though all laws are conjectures not all conjectures are laws. Historical conjectures, as a case in point, are general interpretations of events too complex for a single historical law. What historicists mistakenly think are laws are simply the "patterns" reflecting a selected point of view. Popper grants that to this point his position on the nature of scientific laws does not exclude the search for social and historical laws, though they turn out to be trivial. Popper, however, wants to show that the search for historical laws is in some basic sense incoherent and illegitimate, not merely disappointing. Thus Popper's refutation of even the possibility of historical laws requires another argument. Here Popper must introduce and reinforce the *distinction* between the natural and social sciences, the very distinction he previously denied. Popper's whole idea of a "situational logic" arises as a result of the conclusion that what is specific to social inquiry is the rationality in its object of study.

> The last point seems to me, indeed, to indicate a consider-
> able difference between the natural and the social sciences
> – *perhaps the most important difference in their methods* since
> the other important differences, i.e. specific differences in
> conducting experiments (. . .) and in applying quantitative
> methods (. . .) are differences of degree rather than of kind.
> I refer to the possibility of adopting, in the social sciences,
> what may be called the method of logical or rational
> construction, or perhaps the "zero method." By this I mean
> the method of constructing a model on the assumption
> of complete rationality (and perhaps the assumption of the
> possession of complete information) on the part of all the
> individuals concerned, and of estimating the deviation of
> the actual behaviour of people from the model behaviour,
> using the latter as a kind of zero co-ordinate.[23]

Popper's situational analysis and theory of historical construction
rests on a distinction between reasons and cause. The social
sciences are possible because they seek not a causal explanation
of events but a rational account. Historical understanding cannot
generate universal laws because it seeks to understand the reasons
for actions rather than the causes of events. Popper cites the
historical study, for example, of Giordano Bruno being burned at
the stake for heresy. Understanding operates entirely at the level
of grasping the meaning, reasons, and context which explain the
action, which make it comprehensible. It is not part of such an historical explanation to include "the universal law that all living things
die when exposed to intense heat."[24] Such causal explanations of
events are simply assumed by historical interpretations. But the point
is that the causal level accommodates and cannot discriminate
between any number of historical "points of view," all of which
reflect the "interests or predilections" from which history can be
plotted. Therefore a narrative reconstruction proceeds by reasons
and understanding because it is always overdetermined by causes.

Popper, in the midst of this discussion, does try to once again
salvage his intuitive confidence that there is a single methodology
for all sciences. He suggests that a chemist can be said to be like
a social theorist since a chemist who analyses a compound does
not appeal to universal laws. "His interest is mainly a historical one

– the description of one set of specific events, or of one individual physical body."[25] But the sense of historical in these two cases is very different. While the chemist does ignore laws for purposes of technical or practical efficiency it is not because the object being studied is characterized by rationality, projects, plans, or intentions, any more than a historical reconstruction of Bruno's philosophy is concerned with his "individual physical body."

Popper's point, and it is well to stress it, is that all data requires interpretation, therefore the theoretical selectivity of a point of view is common to both natural and social sciences. But a rational reconstruction is different from chemical analysis. The reconstruction can never achieve the objectivity and neutrality, even in technical or practical application, of chemistry. In the natural sciences there cannot be the same diversity in the interests and viewpoints constitutive of objectivity. Thus the necessity to reconstruct plans, decisions, actions, and strategies as constitutive of the object is peculiar to historical rather than natural objects.

When Popper wants to show how science and historical study are similar he stresses his opposition to empiricism and the constitutive role of evidence for all knowledge.

> All observations are interpreted in the light of theories. Exactly the same holds for documents. Is my return ticket to Paddington a historical document? Yes and no. If I am accused of murder, the ticket may possibly serve to support an alibi, and so become an important historical document. . . . A historical document, like a scientific observation, is a document only relative to a historical problem; and like an observation, it has to be *interpreted*.[26]

But even here Popper's conclusion is that observations in social inquiry cannot be related to universal laws because there is no single perspective from which the documentation is constructed.

> Thus we must not think that a general interpretation can be confirmed by its agreement even with all our records; for we must remember its circularity, as well as the fact that there will always be a number of other (and perhaps incompatible) interpretations that agree with the same records, and that we can rarely obtain new data able to

serve as do crucial experiments in physics. . . .; but if we consider that even in the field of physics . . . new crucial experiments are needed again and again because the old ones are all in keeping with both of two competing and incompatible theories . . . then we shall give up the naive belief that any definite set of historical records can ever be interpreted in one way only.[27]

Popper hopes to clarify what he grants is the "circularity" of interpretation. The reasons and meanings constitutive of historical action are also constitutive of reconstructions. The historical relativity of "problem situations" make all reconstructions provisional. "We can try, conjecturally, to give an *idealized reconstruction of the problem situation in which the agent found himself* [emphasis added], and to that extent make the action 'understandable' – *adequate to the situation as he saw it*" [emphasis added].[28] While such a provisional and constructed perspective holds for all historical studies, including history of science, it is not involved in the study of nature. Since the object of the natural sciences does not have a project, a universal vantage point or interest is possible for understanding it and constituting it as objective.

Popper even concludes, led by his attention to interpretation and understanding, that there cannot be a "criterion" or guideline derived purely from logic or separable from historical problem situations, of truth and rationality. Popper thus admits that there is a kernel of truth in scepticism and relativism. "The kernel of truth is just that there exists no general criterion of truth. But this does not warrant the conclusion that the choice between competing theories is arbitrary."[29] Of course the choice need not be arbitrary even if it is not defined by a single, standard of rationality. If perspective is determined by context, interest, or problem situation then it is neither arbitrary nor universal.

Hilary Putnam has recently also argued against what he calls "criterial conceptions of rationality." Interestingly enough, he considers historicism a case of precisely this error. "I shall call any conception according to which there are institutionalized norms which define what is and is not rationally acceptable a *criterial* conception of rationality."[30] In Putnam's essay "Beyond Historicism," he argues that historicists seek an institutional or sociological account of rationality. This definition of historicism is obviously closer to the second sense of the term that I gave earlier in this chapter. Popper ends up, then, among Putnam's historicists, because in *The Poverty of Historicism* rational strategies are constituted in the final analysis by guidelines or viewpoints *agreed upon* by the scientific community.

It is thus an irony of the history of ideas that Popper's vigorous demonstration of the "poverty" of historicism was actually a propaedeutic to absorbing that rich tradition into his own work. However, Popper resisted recognizing this aspect of his thought. He remained confident that falsification was the definitive rational strategy and thus best answer to scepticism. Finally, against Popper's confidence in a single scientific methodology in the history of science, historicism takes it sweetest revenge – it historicizes it.

3

Conceptual Schemes

There is a thread running through recent epistemology that can be captured by the term "conceptual scheme." I want to show in this chapter why the notion of conceptual schemes led to a revival of historicism, specifically in epistemology and philosophy of science. The term "conceptual scheme" probably has neo-Kantian origins. For example an influential use of the term by P.F. Strawson, as part of what he calls descriptive metaphysics, extended into a study of Kant.[1]

Another example occurs in Rudolf Carnap's essay "Empiricism, Semantics, and Ontology." Carnap distinguishes between internal and external questions about what he called the "frameworks" or languages we use in studying the world.[2] Carnap speaks of, for example, ordinary perceptual judgments about objects as just such a conceptual scheme or framework. Any framework will have internal rules or guidelines for indicating correct and incorrect cases of identification. Carnap distinguishes such "internal" questions about a framework from what he calls an external question. Is the spatio-temporal framework for the identification of things itself the true representation of reality? This question is about the correctness not of individual judgments but of the framework as a whole. Such a question, Carnap argues, cannot be answered because of the way it is formulated. "To be real in the scientific sense means to be an element of the system; hence this concept cannot be meaningfully applied to the system itself."[3] For Carnap there can be no answer to the question of the reality or truth of frameworks since such questions could only emerge internal to a framework. The external questions are thus answered pragmatically. For purposes of utility and efficiency we are free to construct alternative schemes, since accepting, for example, the "framework of things" to solve some problem does not entail believing in the reality of those constructed entities. "To accept the thing world means nothing more than to accept a certain form of language."[4] Carnap's positivism opened up a line of inquiry on this point which would eventually dismantle the orthodox positivist view of science.

An historicist twist on this notion was first made explicit, I believe, in James Conant's *Science and Common Sense*.[5] Conant sought to replace the view of science characteristic of Carnap's positivism with a synthesis of history and philosophy of science. I doubt that there is another book so little read today yet so crucial to understanding how recent issues in philosophy were shaped and formulated.

Conceptual schemes for Conant are the various "fabrics of knowledge" found in the history of scientific knowledge and its dialectical relationship with common sense. Conant seeks to study science not as a formal method but as a strategy of reasoning. "Science is an interconnected series of concepts and conceptual schemes that have developed as a result of experimentation and observation and are fruitful of further experimentation and observation."[6]

Conant's approach made science more speculative than in orthodox philosophy. Science resembled less a formal decision procedure than a "frantic chase of concepts." Conant, to this extent in agreement with positivism, rejects realism. Science does not have access to the correct representation of how the "inanimate world is really constructed." The opposition to realism is, however, not based on a theory of meaning, in Contant, which excludes metaphysical statements. Conant's argument concerns the historicity of the structure constituting objectivity and reality.

In a prophetic comment Conant suggests that "a separate book written by a group of philosophers" would be necessary to treat all the implications of this new conception of science. He defends only in passing his commitment to a cautious and provisional historicism. The dramatic historical shifts and reorganizations of science, not merely at the level of general statements and laws, but even at the level of what are observations and evidence, provide "sufficient justification for treating all scientific theories and explanations as highly provisional."[7]

Conant's book demonstrates this point through what has now become a familiar litany about revolutions in the history of science. However, it would have shocked an attentive contemporary reader. In a series of case studies of conceptual change Conant holds that observations are not the bare, simple constants of experience but historically shaped and molded precisely by different assumptions and theoretical strategies. Conceptual schemes create experiments, not the reverse. Further, conceptual schemes become so habitual that they are identified with a "natural" way of seeing the world. Thus there is an historical link or interaction between science and common sense that explains why certain scientific traditions become difficult to dislodge or reject. An older or challenged conceptual scheme will not be able to be overthrown until there is an alternative. Contrary to the mythic account of the history of science, there are no crucial experiments disapproving older theories and even great scientists have ignored evidence which did not fit the schema holding sway at that time.

I see similarities between the way Conant uses the phrase "conceptual scheme" and such terms that have proliferated in the literature such as "paradigm," "style of reasoning," "discursive formation," "problematic," "third world," and "themata." I do not mean, of course, that all these terms are equivalent. The similarity lies in the effort to study reference or representation only as defined, made possible, or embedded in frameworks which can be viewed as historical traditions rather than logical structures.

Conant gives priority to whole discourses in science over the "things" studied. In fact the notion of a "thing" arises from the way the world is constructed and "read" as an object. This constitution is historical even though it appears fixed and permanent. "For the scientist as for the layman, when they are not on their guard the degree of reality is largely a function of the degree of familiarity with the concept or conceptual scheme; this in turn is a function of the fruitfulness of the idea over a considerable period of time."[8]

The argument is that notions of existence and the reality or truth of statements are not independent of the historical procedures and practices used to construct these different languages. As Hilary

Putnam has recently put the issue; "We have many irreducibly different but legitimate ways of talking, and 'true' existence statements in all of them. To postulate a set of ultimate objects, the furniture of the world . . . whose existence is *absolute*, not relative to our discourse at all . . . is simply to revive the whole failed enterprise of traditional metaphysics."[9]

Conant concludes that there are not only many different schemes but schemes are, for all intents and purposes, immune from direct testing and refutation by counterevidence. As he holds, "the proponents of new conceptual schemes are rarely shaken by a few alleged facts to the contrary."[10] History of science is thus central because the strategies by which schemes succeed, replace opponents, and become part of common sense are not determined by logic or a direct criteria of description. "We have already seen that many scientific ideas have become to deeply embedded in our everyday view of the world that we find it difficult to draw the line between conceptual schemes and matters of fact."[11] Consequently, in what Conant calls "unguarded moments," an identification is automatically made between theoretical statements and what appears as manifest reality. For Conant a statement such as "we live on a globe surrounded by a sea of air" is part of a complex strategy of reasoning reflecting an historical option for the construction of knowledge, rather than recording the given matters of fact.

Conant calls his opposition to scientific realism, certainty, and reference a "skepticism without sneers." By this phrase he means that in treating scientific theories as provisional, historically variable ways of understanding, Conant is not simply "nay saying" every scientific accomplishment. Rather he shifts the study of science from trying to account for the truth of scientific statements, as against unreliable opinions, to investigating how science is formed in a continuum with common sense. In response to those, for example, who insist that the reality of atoms has been amply documented by the success of modern science Conant grants that atoms are designators within a successful framework. But we should not be mislead that this modern conceptualization identifies the real object upon which converge centuries of inquiry. There is no single, final ontology, no *terminus* in science, only that "frantic chase after new concepts." Conant's reconstruction of science, like Popper's, argues against essentialism. Science is not inquiry into the real forces, powers, essences, or causes which assure the correct representation. Beyond the historical vicissitudes of schemes there is no higher judge of what is correct or successful. For Conant even classic philosophical distinctions between what is metaphysical and what is empirical, or between mind and body, are so many strategies within traditions. Each distinction is an interpretive "move," and thus a matter, not of purely methodological debate, but of historical interests and context.

Conant is suspicious of what appears obvious or natural. The manifest and apparent are the interpretive "paths" that have survived, proved fruitful, and become embedded. Any schema becomes eventually a habitual routine of interpretation. It silently becomes identified with reality and whatever is both obvious and natural. In that way habits in interpretation appear to mirror the natural world. Conant's stress on schemes as one path among many, as the realization of only one historical possibility, is intended to break this identification with nature and therefore the undeserved authority and certainty that certain frameworks acquire.

Thomas Kuhn, a student of Conant, developed these arguments into a new approach to the history of science which emphasized the multiple alternative accounts for any *"prescribed* list of observations."

> A scientist's willingness to use a conceptual scheme in explanations is an index of his commitment to the scheme, a token of his belief that his model is the only valid one. Such commitment or belief is always rash, because economy and cosmological satisfaction cannot guarantee truth, whatever "truth" may mean. The history of science is cluttered with the relics of conceptual schemes that were once fervently believed and that have since been replaced by incompatible theories. There is no way of proving that a conceptual scheme is final.[12]

For Kuhn the importance of history of science lies in the fact that the "paths" of inquiry are not laid out by logical or methodological procedures. They result from, even when formulated as methodological guidelines, cultural conventions. With "routinization" the study of nature becomes embedded and, therefore, from inside a historical context, seems automatic. Different traditions of inquiry create controversies about truth and rationality. But these debates can never be resolved by observations which contradict or confirm theories or beliefs based on logical methods. What supervenes over both are the traditions themselves, the "styles" or languages of inquiry that are constructed external to science.

> Our immediate problem, however, is the analysis of the grip exerted upon men's minds by the ancient tradition of astronomical research. How could this tradition provide a set of mental grooves that guided the astronomical imagination, limited the conceptions available in research, an made certain sorts of innovations difficult to conceive and more difficult to accept? . . . A conviction of this sort is difficult to break, particularly once it has been embodied in the practice of a whole generation of astronomers who transmit it to their successors through their teaching and writing. . . . Fundamental astronomical concepts had become strands in a far larger fabric of thought, and the nonastronomical strands could be as important as the astronomical in binding the imagination of astronomers.[13]

The metaphor of a "fabric" of thought binding a world view together suggests another source for the notion of conceptual schemes. In a famous criticism of the positivist dualism of analytic and synthetic statements, "Two Dogmas of Empiricism," W.V.O. Quine argues that empirical statements do not directly confront the world nor are they dictated by experience alone.[14] As already seen in Carnap's version of positivism, any statements that do not arise solely from experience must either be analytically true, mere conventions of word use, or meaningless because they are poorly formulated. Though such statements look normal there is no way to determine their truth or falsity. For this reason Carnap relegated external questions about frameworks to metaphysics and thus a matter of pragmatism rather than truth. Quine calls this distinction a "dogma of empiricism." In dislodging it Quine shows that conventional word use is parasitical on experience while, symmetrically, empirical claims are partly conventional and therefore somewhat autonomous from experience. "The totality of our so-called knowledge . . . *is a man-made fabric* [emphasis added] which impinges on experience only along the edges."[15] What Quine calls the "underdetermination" of theories means that statements refer, not by direct access to the world, but through systems of "irreducible posits" which introduce entities into "our conception only as cultural posits."

Quine's conception of knowledge as a system protected against revision excludes, along with the positivist theory of meaning, Popper's falsification. Systems of concepts allow for and depend on a loose fit between concept and world. Hence, as with Conant, Quine allows for many possible alternative schemes. There is no way to fix the reference of our concepts, to secure a permanent and independent measure of "match" between concepts and world. Reference, in Quine's words, is "inscrutable."

One effect of using conceptual schemes, as Quine and Conant do, is a weakened distinction between scientific and non-scientific inquiry. In Conant's historical approach there is constant mediation between science and common sense and no distinctive method for gaining knowledge. Conant simply points to the inherent complexity of scientific history and what he calls "the stumbling way in which even the ablest of the scientists in every generation has had to fight through the thickets of erroneous observations, misleading generalizations, inadequate formulations, and unconscious prejudice."[16] If there were a single method by which such inquiry succeeded an examination of the history of any science would have revealed it long ago.

Paul Feyerabend's *Against Method* is the most recent extension of Conant's historicism to the very notion of rationality.[17] Philosophy of science does not discover or justify methodological guidelines for the growth of knowledge, but unmasks and criticizes the strategic or rhetorical devices used in history to support scientific hypotheses. Feyerabend does not intend to denigrate philosophy. He considers that such a flexible and loose idea of reasoning is precisely the key to understanding how specific paths for the production of knowledge are made through history's range of possibilities.

Recently Ian Hacking has suggested "a relativist problem from the heartland of rationality" for both orthodox pictures of rationality and refutations of scepticism. Though the connection between historicism and relativism will return as a theme in my concluding chapter, Hacking's summary helps to situate the historicist tendencies of recent epistemology and the motivation for Feyerabend's radical conclusions about the role of history in the formation of knowledge.

Hacking suggests as a relativist position within modern theory of knowledge and history of science. First is the view of reason as a kind of "style" with its own patterns of growth and replacement. These "styles of reasoning" are replaced or retained not under the pressure of logical consistency or truth and falsity but as expressions of deeper world views. Hacking suggests that for this new relativism the standards of truth and falsity are themselves produced by such a style of reasoning. These points lead, in Hacking's conclusion to an explicit historicism. "Hence many categories of possibility, of what may be true or false, *are contingent upon historical events*, namely the development of certain styles of reasoning."[18]

Traditionally when philosophers confront the possibility of such alternative systems of reasoning they assume first that all reasoning must be at its base the same. But that means that alternatives are only treated as meaningful if they reflect the conception of method employed in the philosopher's present. Thus the introduction of historicity into this problem has a corrosive effect on evaluative judgments. The point of producing histories of science is no longer the traditional project of showing how much knowledge has progressed but a sceptical and relativist strategy for undermining current certainties.

Feyerabend's study treats good arguments as the result of interpretive traditions rather than logic. Feyerabend argues that in establishing or defending a new scientific theory the defender is never confronted with specific or discrete objections but with a total resistance to the new scheme. Conversely the revolutionary must treat the old theory as wrong "root and branch." The factual data from an older tradition acts as a "mental block" against change because old data, observation, and reasoning is "contaminated" with such obstacles as the "obvious" or what is "natural." Knowledge is the sedimentation of tradition.[19]

Feyerabend's central example of historical argument is Galileo's opposition to Aristotelianism. Galileo had to make the idea of a moving earth thinkable in view of its inconsistency with long established facts, everyday observations, and existing science and philosophy. As Feyerabend stresses, philosophers of science have often concluded that the "reasonable" strategy is to preserve as much of "established" knowledge as possible. Thus from this standard of rationality Galileo should have striven to preserve the immense Aristotelian system and reject the hypothesis of a moving earth. Given such a method of science Galileo's actual strategy was unscientific. But, as Feyerabend holds, that applies judgments about science retrospectively, from the hindsight possible in the present as to what constitutes science or reason. Thus the existing conceptions of rational and normal procedures in science are implicitly historicist. What Galileo actually did, Feyerabend argues, violated rational conservation and proceeded "counterinductively." Galileo asked himself what would have to change if Copernicanism were true and thus constructed "natural interpretations" in defense of a new system.

The fundamental issue for Galileo's new physics was the relationship of the moving earth hypothesis to the observation of motion on earth. Copernicus had shown that a moving earth, a moving observatory, changed the explanation of certain astronomical events, for example the retrograde motion of the planets. But Galileo began to argue, analogically, that a moving earth would alter explanations of moving bodies on the earth, a notorious weak point of Aristotelianism.

A famous argument against the moving earth was that a body dropped from a height should fall behind the point at which it had been dropped since, during the time of the fall, the earth moved. The "fact" that the object fell straight down, as directly observed, was manifest evidence that the earth was a rest. Galileo could have denied the validity of sense experience. While such a strategy was reasonable, Feyerabend holds, such a drastic argument would turn against Galileo's own use of experiment. Therefore Galileo changed the "natural interpretation" of such motion through various metaphors and analogies which tried gradually to embed a new conceptual scheme.

Galileo argued that though the senses are valid instruments for gathering knowledge they can only record relative motions. This relativity of motion accounts for the inability to perceive the earth as moving and to perceive the relative motions involved in the tower argument. Though Galileo produced ingenious examples of everyday events in which the motion of one body only appears relative to another, and in which motion may be imperceptible when viewed from another moving body, these were analogies resting on a new and untested conceptual change. Galileo's strategy established a *new observation language*, and thus a new conceptual domain. But Galileo makes the arguments appear more persuasive by pretending that his analogies are about what is apparent, natural, and manifest common sense. Thus in Feyerabend's account, Galileo defended relative motion not by logic, method, or truth but, first, by simply demonstrating how this idea helps to support the Copernican theory and, second, by claiming to find support in common sense. "Galileo introduces the principle [of circular inertia], again not by reference to experiment or to independent observation, but by reference to what everybody is already supposed to know."[20]

Feyerabend's conclusion is that Galileo's reasoning was a combination of rhetoric and propaganda.[21] Illicit strategies of argument produced "good" science. In fact Feyerabend concludes that any such scientific creativity requires that inquiry be treated as relative and historical. Therefore Aristotle's model of explanation now appears unnatural and unscientific, not because it violates some basic rules, but as an effect of historical sedimentation. A new conceptual scheme relegates past traditions to irrelevance by changing the "natural interpretations." Method enforces an amnesia concerning the history of reason. Though Feyerabend is sympathetic to Galileo the point is not to make him a prophet of modern science. Galileo created historical possibilities of inquiry, whatever his intent was, which cannot be judged by convergence toward the truth. Objectivity is also historical.

Feyerabend's arguments collide with both the realist and phenomenalist positions in current philosophy of science. By studying science as series of historical shifts in conceptual schemes Feyerabend makes the distinction between the theoretical and the observational, or between internal and external questions, relative.[22] Phenomenalism, for example, assumes that observations are non-controversial claims, easily isolated from the theories they are supposed to support. Therefore the phenomenalist position restricts science to a study of experience with no speculative assumptions about the nature of reality. Against this position the traditional realist view stresses that science allows for ontological commitments which are the result of the entire theory rather than discrete observations.

This new historicism implicit in Feyerabend's attack is friendly to neither view. It is not a version of realism since it treats the object of inquiry as an historical *concept*. The real is defined by the framework. But arguments like Feyerabend's also hold that what appears is not naturally given but constructed. Observations cannot adjudicate between alternative schemes. Because the approach to science associated with the historical study of schemes differs from both current positions in philosophy of science, and yet offers no certain standards or viewpoints from which to judge and evaluate knowledge claims, it has been linked, by critics, to a revival of idealism, scepticism, or relativism. The slogan that the history of concepts or ideas just *is* reality seems Hegelian. Historical relativism emerges because perceptions and conceptions are inseparable parts of a single framework.[23] Instead of different scientific theories being about or referring to the same reality or thing we have the argument that reference is constructed or constituted by a broader framework or style. Frameworks and their production of a style of reasoning are historical contingencies. The object of knowledge is culturally constructed.

Whenever there emerges a renewed interest in the history of science similar issues follow. For example, Pierre Duhem's famous study *The Aim and Structure of Physical Theory*, was in part motivated by his effort to rethink the historical transition from medieval to modern physics and astronomy.[24] Duhem utilized the metaphor of "reading" to describe the way in which experiment relates to observation. For example, in minutely observing the oscillation of a piece of iron in a specific experimental situation the physicist simply *sees* electrical resistance, not just the oscillation. But to understand what "electrical resistance" means we will need to know when the observation was made and what theoretical account held sway. Such activities of measurement theoretically construct domains of evidence, rather than wait for the direct presence of a special experience. The experiment is not interested in the objects themselves and thus the objects are marginal. Only the theoretical interpretation or conceptual object of inquiry is central. Electricity, in the absence of a theory which "conceptualizes" current, is neither an experience nor a natural object. Objects outside of all concepts are, as Duhem so nicely puts it, "dead letters."

> But, once again, what the physicist states as the result of an experiment is not the recital of observed facts, but the interpretation and the transposition of these facts into the ideal, abstract, symbolic world created by theories he regards as established.[25]

Between theories and facts there can never be an ultimate parity, matching, or correspondence since any given state of affairs accommodates multiple theoretical interpretations.

> There can be no adequation between the precise and rigorous theoretical fact and the practical fact with vague and uncertain contours such as our perceptions reveal in everything. That is why the same practical fact can correspond to an infinity of theoretical facts.[26]

Duhem's position implies that the domain of evidence is not constant throughout the history of science. There has been a great deal of recent debate in philosophy of science about how to preserve the neutrality of observation statements and therefore their use in science.[27] The position I am summarizing now does not exclude the *use* of observation statements. But it does exclude a non-controversial use of such claims, or more precisely it argues that our senses, along with our concepts, are historial.

A theme associated with this conceptual scheme approach to science could be called the "ambiguity of discovery." I want to give a more extended example which brings together the implicit discussion here on the historicity of experience.

Most historians of science consider Antoine Lavoisier's discovery of oxygen as the most significant historical event in the emergence of modern chemistry. Interestingly, one of the earliest uses of Lavoisier as an example was in Engels's introduction to Volume II of *Capital* where, defending Marx against accusations that Marxist economics was derivative of classical political economy, Engels compared Marx's intellectual revolution to Lavoisier's discovery of oxygen.

I begin with Thomas Kuhn's historicist warning about the nature of Lavoisier's famous discovery.

> Though undoubtedly correct, the sentence "Oxygen was discovered," misleads by suggesting that discovering something is a single simple act assimilable to our usual (and also questionable) concept of seeing. That is why we so readily assume that discovering, like seeing or touching, should be unequivocally attributable to an individual and to a moment in time . . . But if both observation and conceptualization, fact and assimilation to theory, are inseparably linked in discovery, then discovery is a process and must take time. Only when all the relevant conceptual categories are prepared in advance . . . can discovering *that* and discovering *what* occur effortlessly, together, and in an instant.[28]

The revolution in chemistry associated with Antoine Lavoisier has at least three possible locations. First, there is Lavoisier's own claim that he did a crucial experiment in 1772 with sulphur and phosphorus which led him to reject the then current account of combustion. Second, there are the several experiments which produced a gas of disputed name by different persons (Scheele, Priestly, and Lavoisier) between 1774–1778. Finally there is the publication of Lavoisier's *Traité élémentaire do chimie* which supplies a theory of chemical elements and nomenclature precisely situating the term oxygen.

The context of all these events was the presence of a theory of chemistry called phlogiston chemistry. The term phlogiston (from the Greek "to burn") was part of a theory which systematized the traditional four elements view of nature. It accepted that there were earthy, firey, watery, and airy substances and specified that something called phlogiston accounted for combustion. All chemical reactions were transformations of these four fundamental natures. In combustion, for example, a body gave off its firey principle, phlogiston, and left behind an ash or earthy residue. Bodies rich in phlogiston, such as charcoal, burn a long time. Since a body gives of phlogiston during combustion, combustion will stop when a body is in an enclosed space. The explanation that the enclosed air can only absorb so much phlogiston showed the reality of this hypothesized substance.

Phlogiston chemistry was able to connect two seemingly unrelated reactions with the same underlying principles. Smelting is the process whereby an ore, which is an "earthy" substance in phlogiston theory, generates a metal through combustion by the addition of charcoal (a rich source of phlogiston). Phlogiston chemists saw this reaction as a reversal of ordinary combustion. In combustion phlogiston is given off by the burning body whereas in smelting the phlogiston, supplied by the charcoal, is absorbed by the ore and results in a metal. Metals shine because they contain the firey substance phlogiston. Phlogiston based chemistry revealed hidden symmetries in these natural reactions.

Phlogiston chemistry could also claim significant explanatory power. Respiration, for example, gave off heat and thus was a kind of combustion. The air given off through the mouth was appropriately saturated with phlogiston and did not support further combustion or respiration when collected and tested. The body took in phlogiston-free air to bring about the combustion within itself, and thus expell the highly phlogisticated, "fixed air" (a general term of the time used, among other things, to refer to carbon monoxide). Even the rusting of metal could be considered a slow motion combustion reaction since phlogiston was slowly released into the air (the phlogiston which had previously formed the metal during smelting) and the metal returned to its earthy state.

In 1772 Lavoisier deposited a sealed note with the French Academy in which he noted that sulphur and phosphorous gained weight during combustion. The note states that the weight gain is due to a "prodigous quantity of air that is fixed during combustion and combines with vapors. . . . I am persuaded that the increase in weight of metallic calxes is due to the same cause."[29] If metals gain weight during combustion there is a discrepancy with phlogiston theory which claims that a burning body looses phlogiston during that reaction (and only gains during smelting). How could the loss of phlogiston produce a gain in weight?

The weight gain problem had been recognized by the phlogiston chemists before Lavoisier's note. In a recent article Alan Musgrave argues that weight gain was not, in itself, fatal to phlogiston chemistry because the older theory could be modified by auxiliary assumptions to handle that particular discrepancy.[30] For example, it might be supposed that while a body gives off phlogiston during combustion it also gains weight by absorbing "fixed air" in the atmosphere and some water. There was also the argument that phlogiston had "negative weight." That would explain both the weight gain and the phenomena of lighter-than-air balloons.

Also events do not bear out the interpretation that Lavoisier, at the time of the original note, really saw the discrepancy as fatal to phlogiston theory. Actually there were three sealed notes and only the third one rejects phlogiston chemistry. At the time of the first sealed note Lavoisier was a phlogiston chemist, with reservations. He was pursuing a lead, suggested by the famous Joseph Priestly, that the weight gain was due to fixed air. As Lavoisier moved to an anti-phlogiston position and a protracted battle with the phlogistonists, around 1778, he streamlined the story of his discovery and pushed it back to the earliest note.

Lavoisier's attitude here reveals the role of residual or implicit philosophical assumptions in scientific discovery. Baconian empiricism, which Lavoisier appealed to in defense of his views, equates discovery with the act of seeing. Therefore in Lavoisier's own account of his discovery he had to remove any hesitancy in his perception of the facts. While, originally, Lavoisier thought weight gain was compatible with phlogiston chemistry, later he made it appear that this "fact" led directly and simply to his new theory. Lavoisier treated "oxygen" as though its discovery only required open eyes.

The dispute about the discovery of oxygen occurred because it was produced, under laboratory conditions, by more than one experimenter. Priestly, a lifelong committed phlogiston chemist, called the new air "dephlogisticated air" – whereas Lavoisier would eventually decide on the term oxygen, to insert the air into a wider revolution in chemistry theory and nomenclature. Until then he called it "eminently respirable air." The term "oxygen" was selected because it was Greek for "begets an acid" since Lavoisier had mistakenly concluded that all acids have oxygen in them.

There is evidence that Lavoisier learned how to produce oxygen from Priestly.[31] The famous experiment involved producing a gas by smelting mercury, a gas which was then reabsorbed when the mercury burned. On a trip to Paris Priestly reported on experiments with the red calx of mercury. This calx could be reduced without the use of charcoal. Priestly concluded that the "fixed air" which does not support combustion comes from charcoal. The use of red calx of mercury allowed for an experiment in which a calx reduces without the addition of charcoal and fixed air. Interestingly, the same experiment that turned Lavoisier away from phlogiston only confirmed Priestly in his belief in the theory.

Priestly reported, possibly to Lavoisier, that in the reduction of the red calx in air with a burning lens the product was not "fixed air" but a new kind of air which supports combustion much better than ordinary air. Priestly chose to call this air "dephlogisticated," precisely because of its purity. In 1775 Lavoisier writes concerning his replication of Priestly's experiment;

> From the fact that common air changes to fixed air when combined with charcoal it would seem natural to conclude that fixed air is nothing but a combination of common air and phlogiston. This is Mr. Priestly's opinion and it must be admitted that it is not without probability; however, when one looks into the facts in detail, contradictions arise so frequently I feel it is necessary to ask philosophers and chemists to suspend judgement; I hope to be soon in a position to communicate the reasons for my doubts.[32]

While expressing reservations, Lavoisier's statement (written at about the same time as the first sealed note) remains committed to the phlogiston reactions as probable. But when Lavoisier revised his discovery in 1778 the same text was changed to read:

> Since charcoal disappears completely in the revivification of the mercury calx and since only mercury and fixed air are produced by this operation, one is forced to conclude that the principle to which hitherto has been given the name fixed air is the result of the combination of the eminently respirable part of the air with charcoal; and this is what I propose to develop in a more satisfactory manner in subsequent memoirs which I shall devote to this object.[33]

Lavoisier has taken a more aggressive stance in reporting his experimental results. But the aggression follows not from observations but as a result of a new theory. Lavoisier constructed an account in which phlogiston played no role and combustion only required eminently respirable air. Once Lavoisier decided that weight gain was critical and resulted in a precise reduction of respirable air during the experiment, only the fixed air from the calx needed to be explained.

In his first version Lavoisier noted that charcoal played a role and claimed Priestly's account was probably correct. In the second version Lavoisier was boldly "forced to conclude" that fixed air was released by the charcoal burning in respirable air. Without using the word "oxygen" Lavoisier took the conceptual step. He changed schemes and thus both the object of explanation and the problem.

The story continues ironically, since Priestly, after receiving a copy of Lavoisier's first version, noted that Lavoisier misused a nitrous air test that Priestly had designed to measure the "goodness" of air. Priestly stressed that the nitrous air tested showed that the new air was not atmospheric air but a qualitatively different air. Correcting this error in part led to Lavoisier's more dramatic interpretation of the experiment. Once again, what Priestly saw as a refinement of phlogiston concepts Lavoisier saw as their demise.

It is fascinating that Priestly, defender of the phlogiston chemistry, would point out to the revolutionary Lavoisier that the air produced was, in fact, a new air and that atmospheric air was a compound rather than an element. We associate those two views now with Lavoisier's new chemistry. The fact that they could coexist with the phlogiston theory suggests that a conceptual scheme, by having central and marginal claims, is more flexible and rationally salvageable than traditional history of science assumes. In conclusion, it is hopeless to ask who made the first discovery of oxygen since the difference between oxygen and dephlogisticated air is not a matter of words or perceptions, but a difference in conceptual schemes. Conceptual schemes are constructed, not discovered.

Engels used this case study to make an analogy between the discovery of oxygen and the discovery of surplus value by Marx. Engels emphasized that Marx distinguished surplus value from rent, profit, and interest. As Louis Althusser describes Marx's procedure;

> When Marx reads them [classical economists] he re-estab-
> lishes this missing word in their texts: surplus value. This
> act of re-establishing an absent word may seem insignifi-
> cant, but it has considerable theoretical consequences:
> in fact, this word is not a word, but a *concept*, and a
> theoretical concept, which is here the *representative* of a
> new conceptual system, the correlative of the appearance
> of a new object.[34]

These comments could apply equally to the phlogiston case. In revising a scheme it will always appear, to outsiders or opponents, that the effort is a quibble about words. But, as Engels saw, there is a deeper analogy between the oxygen and surplus value examples. I began this discussion with a quote from Kuhn to the effect that the Lavoisier revolution was an ideal example of a change in conceptual order rather than a triumph of observational acumen. That point is born out by the multiple laboratory discoveries, under each scheme. Engels made the same argument in defense of Marx's discovery.

Engels was replying, in the preface to Volume II of *Capital*, to charges that Marx had "robbed" his theory from Johann Karl Rodbertus, a minor German economist of the time. Engels replies that classical political economy is Marx's object of critical scrutiny. Marx's discoveries cannot be understood except within the context of his theoretical opposition. Since Rodbertus is a second rate expositor of classical political economy, it could appear, to the naive reader, that Marx borrows from him.

To elucidate this point, Engels suggests an example from the history of chemistry. He recounts the multiple discoveries of oxygen under different names and stresses that the name "dephlogisticated air" acted to resist conceptual innovation.

> Priestly and Scheele had produced oxygen without know-
> ing what they had laid their hands on. They remained
> prisoners of the phlogistic categories as they came down
> to them.[35]

Engels emphasizes that the event in the laboratory, the production of a new gas, did not in itself produce a shift in the conceptual scheme. In fact the phlogistic categories were capable of finding a place for this new event. Being a "prisoner" of these categories, as Engels calls it, was seeing dephlogisticated air while producing something that would be called "oxygen" in another scheme. Thus Engels concludes; "the element which was destined to upset all phlogistic views and to revolutionise chemistry remained barren in their hands."

Engels's point is very subtle. For phlogiston chemistry, the new air was not a radical discovery. It might require some modification in the overall theory – for example, Priestly was prepared to abandon the view that air was an element – but discovering a new "air" actually *strengthened* the overall theory; it served as a sign of progress. With a change in concepts, however, both the problem situation and thus the nature of observations changed.

> Thus [Lavoisier] was the first to place all chemistry, which in its phlogistic form had stood on its head, squarely on its feet. And although he did not produce oxygen simultaneously and independently of the others, as he later claimed, he nevertheless is the real discoverer of oxygen *vis-a-vis* the others who only produced it without knowing what they had produced.[36]

Engels notes that Lavoisier's later claim to priority is naive since Lavoisier then equates discovery with the act of observation in the laboratory. Lavoisier thinks he can only be the discoverer of oxygen if he "saw" it first. Engels agrees that Lavoisier is the real discoverer, but under conditions Lavoisier would not understand.

First, Lavoisier is the real discoverer *vis-a-vis* the others, meaning that his conceptual shift is only a revolution in a context. For there to be a breakthrough there must be an obstacle, another theory against which to articulate the conceptual shift. Deciding if Lavoisier is the true discoverer of oxygen requires specifying the historical context. Outside of such a context answers are ambiguous. Second, Engels argues that Lavoisier discovers not a "thing" in the sense of an object in the laboratory – the same "thing" in Priestly's lab for instance – but a "concept" which was missing in Priestly's theory.

The point Engels is building towards is an analogy with Marx's discovery of "surplus value." Marx "named" something that was present in classical political economy, albeit in a "dephlogisticated" form. Those who equate discovery with producing the "real object" assume that there is no radical difference between Marx and classical political economy since they both saw "surplus" but named it differently. But the shift between theories is the key point – just as the presence of oxygen in the laboratories of the phlogiston chemists did not lessen the revolution in Lavoisier's discovery. For Engels, revolutions in science occur not around real objects but around the problem situations. Engels continues:

> And [Marx] took a view directly opposite to that of all his predecessors. What they regarded as a *solution*, he considered but a *problem* . . . that here it was not simply a matter of stating as economic fact (*einer ökonomischen Tatsache*) . . . but of explaining a fact which was destined to revolutionize all economics. . . . With this fact as his starting point he examined all the economic categories (*die sämtlichen vorgefundenen Kategorien*) which he found at hand, just as Lavoisier proceeding from oxygen had examined the categories of phlogiston chemistry which he found at hand.[37]

The distinction throughout this passage is between the fact (*Tatsache*) and the categorical scheme (*die sämtlichen vorgefundenen Kategorien*). Facts are inseparable from categorical schemes.

A theoretical revolution always concerns the whole conceptual scheme and not some discrete statement of fact. In a view like Pierre Duhem's the simple "statement" of a fact cannot overthrow a conceptual arrangement. Hence, discoveries are never acts of seeing what someone else failed to see. The existing facts only emerge because the categorical scheme accommodates them. Experiment is only crucial when already embedded in a scheme. Finally, discovery is always in relation to opposing conceptions. There must be at least two discourses for there to be breakthrough. Theory is in part the criticism of predecessors: a textual and historical treatment. One theorizes against other texts, other theories, other explanations, other representations – never against the blank, given world.

4

Rational Reconstruction

Before looking more deeply at the sceptical and relativist implications of the second sense of historicism I need to consider in more detail whether there is not a version of Popper's approach which could avoid relativism. Clearly Popper thought that rational reconstruction would do more than merely recount or describe historical events. Are there no necessary criteria of rationality built into the reconstruction and constitution of historical interpretations? Is not the history of science precisely where such universal standards of rationality are to be found? To answer these questions we need a more developed account of rational reconstruction.

I have emphasized the historicist side to the original idea of reconstruction because it embeds rational strategies within traditions and problem situations. But I have equally argued that we must already come to the study of history with some idea of rationality by which an account is constructed. If historical narratives are constructed rather than described then we should, as Popper suggested, be able to judge the resulting narratives of interpretations by some standards.

I turn here to Imre Lakatos, a critical follower of Popper's broad philosophical concerns, who integrates historiography into the theory of knowledge, and therefore expands Popper's idea of a rational reconstruction.

For Lakatos science cannot be studied as some simple ahistorical activity. What we call science is the historical rise and fall of intellectual traditions. These diverse traditions whose clash and growth are the object of reconstructions are what Lakatos calls "research programmes." Lakatos applies the term research program very broadly. It covers anything from Biblical hermeneutics to astronomy. To the extent that we are interested in knowledge as historical the specific subject matter cannot be used to judge whether a tradition is rational or scientific. The idea of research programs stresses that rationality concerns the overall evolution of a tradition, its responses to successes and failures in context, and its historical alternatives. Short of such a reconstruction there is no shorthand way to determine whether a certain inquiry is rational, or scientific, or even fruitful. Neither a purely logical analysis nor theoretical correspondence with reality will replace the inherent historicity of knowledge claims. If there is a distinction between scientific and unscientific knowledge, or rational growth versus accidental discovery – and Lakatos believes there are such distinctions – then it will lie in the "patterns" by which the history of inquiry is modified.

Lakatos distinguishes between a set of beliefs that constitute the core, or central dogma of the tradition, and a looser series of peripheral claims that surround and support that central view.[1] Lakatos claims that any tradition of inquiry will develop a "negative heuristic." That means a set of procedures or rules whose purpose is to protect and prevent a direct refutation by experience of the doctrine's core conception. The reason for the "negative heuristic" is that any tradition, such as atomism or physiological reduction, is so speculative that it would be struck down immediately by its inconsistency with a great deal of experience. On strictly logical grounds all research programs are improbable and riddled with problems. To protect the hope that the tradition will generate valuable research we must protect it, by convention, from falsification through crucial experiments. Consequently, in Lakatos's reconstructions of the history of science crucial experiments are always mythical.[2]

Within any research program there is also a "positive heuristic." By this term, Lakatos means that any tradition will have exemplars of its successes, admissible problems and protocols or procedures for getting solutions to problems. The positive heuristic is a program's pedagogy. Thus, taking these two more specific clarifications of what is meant by a research program Lakatos concludes that the history of science is the history of these traditions. We study not single theories but groups or series of theories going through adjustments and modifications through conventional procedures. The aim of all these modifications is to preserve the central doctrine and yet generate some solutions or empirical support for that account of the world. Whether a given program can be said to produce knowledge about the world is an historical question. Further, there is no quick answer. The diagnosis of a research program's fate is a drawn out, imprecise affair with the occasional dramatic deathbed recovery; normally, burial occurs after a lingering illness.

While Lakatos treats the epistemologist as an historian studying the production of evidence, observations and tests in context, that does not mean a research program is insulated from all dissonance. This turn to history by Lakatos does not mean that all traditions are equally close to the truth. In doing the historical work of reconstruction Lakatos seeks a philosophical goal, namely whether or not a tradition has "degenerated" in its production of knowledge. Lakatos does believe that through such study a universal account of what it means for science to progress and claim knowledge will emerge. Such an account of reason and knowledge will be a sophisticated and historical account (as opposed to some instant logical analysis) but will reach some definitive conclusions about the nature of human knowledge.

As I have stressed, Lakatos's turn to history concerns in part the realization that knowledge is the product of traditions which require time to flourish and defend themselves. A tradition needs to translate its central speculation about reality into the specific issues, problems, and questions that we normally think of as research. Without a "cushion," a research program would be reduced to empty but grand assertions about reality, but no inquiry. Inquiry contains the inevitable "tinkering" with the peripheral claims and perhaps eventually the core doctrine itself – but always toward a growth in knowledge through the solution of its ever varying problem situations.

Lakatos, however, differs from the normal historian of science. He restricts the historical study to what he calls "internal" change. By that term Lakatos wants to exclude from the historicity of knowledge the various religious, political, or aesthetic factors that historians often stress. I will discuss this distinction between internal and external aspects in more detail shortly, but it rests on making the reconstruction as ideal as possible. Though scientific decisions, for example, undoubtedly respond to psychological or sociological influences Lakatos does not consider those aspects "explanatory" of the production of knowledge. What Lakatos has in mind when he excludes the "external" histories of knowledge are, for instance, arguments like Thomas Kuhn's: that the study of scientific revolutions should include investigations of such factors as calendar reform, theological debates, and political and economic changes in the society. In Lakatos's view, all these kinds of factors are irrelevant to historical reconstruction. Lakatos states;

> [I]nternal history is self-sufficient for the presentation of the history of disembodied science, including de-generating problemshifts. External history explains why some people have false beliefs about scientific progress, and how their scientific activity may be influenced by such beliefs.[3]

The reason Lakatos puts so much stress on excluding externalities in the historical study of knowledge is that he wants a critical rather than an anecdotal or antiquarian history. The history of knowledge exemplifies normative standards. A rational reconstruction is no mere description of what happened, no matter how broadly conceived. Lakatos argues that to the extent that historical narratives become purely descriptive they must abandon all evaluative standards. But the point of a narrative is to explain why something occurred and therefore rests on some theory of knowledge. A research program is not simply *there* in the history of science as a documented fact, but is more like a Weberian ideal type. It is the idea of the program or tradition that tells us what to look for in history. For Lakatos, then, theory of science is, at bottom, theory of history. "This shifting of the *locus* of scientific appraisal from propositions to problemshifts introduced a historical dimension into a scientific appraisal."[4]

In an effort to throw more light on these abstracts concepts, I will use one of Lakatos's more accessible case studies, namely the Copernican revolution.[5] While it is an overworked example it provides us with concrete details for understanding his theory of the connection between history and knowledge and, as such, is useful. In Lakatos's version of events, the hypothesis that the earth is the unmoving center of the universe "migrated" through different research programs. According to him, the geocentric hypothesis only gradually became a central dogma. Thus, by the time of Copernicus it was this central conception that was the object of controversy. Lakatos claims that geocentrism became a central dogma only in the late Middle Ages, after the Ptolemaic system and Aristotelian cosmology were unified within Christian theology.

According to Lakatos the older traditions of astronomy did not necessarily emphasize geocentrism. In fact, the hard core of astronomy had originally been what was called the "Platonic heuristic," namely the view that all orbits must be circular and uniform in motion. In ancient astronomy the Platonic heuristic was dogma, while the geocentric hypothesis was treated as an auxiliary hypothesis depending on whether it did a better or worse job in preserving circularity and uniformity in the orbits. Copernicus is thus pictured in Lakatos's account as reviving the ancient research tradition or Platonic heuristic against the Ptolemaic dogma of geocentrism. Ptolemaic astronomy is attacked for not preserving the uniformity and circularity of orbits.

The Copernican revolution thus had an internal historical "logic." It was the internal shift of hard cores in these research traditions rather than the politics, institutions, culture, or aesthetics which explains the revolution as an intellectual event. Even though ancient astronomers prior to Copernicus had hypothesized that the earth moves, we now see, as a result of Lakatos's narrative, that those assertions functioned within radically different contexts. Copernicus faced a program – the theoretical construct invented by Lakatos's narrative – in which the geocentric hypothesis was a dogma, the metaphysical hard core of Ptolemaic-Aristotelian cosmology. Therefore Lakatos must do more than simply point to cultural differences, he must show, if this was a rational and scientific modification, that the Ptolemaic-Aristotelian program was degenerating and that Copernicus's revival of the Platonic heuristic was a progressive internal problemshift.[6]

> Copernicus did not create a completely new programme;
> he revived the Aristarchian version of the Platonic pro-
> gramme. The hard core of the programme is the proposi-
> tion that the stars provide the primary frame of reference
> for physics. Copernicus did not invent a new heuristic
> but attempted to restore and rejuvenate the Platonic
> one. (p. 182).

In Lakatos's reading, the statement that "the earth moves" functions
relative to a research tradition. Hypotheses are too small a unit by
which to appraise a tradition. What the epistemologist must judge
is the entire program, at the level of a tradition. Only at that
the historical level can the distinction between degenerating and
progressive patterns be decided.

In the Ptolemaic-Aristotelian tradition geocentrism became, as
Lakatos reconstructs it, the central dogma and therefore that
tradition was willing to sacrifice or weaken the Platonic heuristic.
The Ptolemaic system was just such a compendium of devices, such
as the eccentric (displacing the earth from the center of its orbit) or
the epicycle (giving the planet a lopping path that allowed for overall
non-circularity) – each of which preserved an unmoving earth by
tinkering with the conditions for defining circularity and uniformity
in the movements of the planets. For example, Ptolemy was able to
translate these conditions into purely mathematical fictions rather
than motions that really must occur. It was the program, not
nature, which pushed, directed, and constrained theory. A rational
reconstruction must judge these dictated patterns and decide
whether the strategic conventions led to growth of knowledge.
Lakatos's critical history leads to the conclusion that Copernicus's
program was superior, i.e. more rational and progressive than
the degenerating Ptolemaic system. The new Copernican strategy
resulted in theoretical, empirical, and heuristic growth.

> [Copernicus' programme] predicted a wider range of
> phenomena, it was corroborated by novel facts and, in
> spite of the degenerative elements of *De Revolutionibus* it
> had more heuristic unity than the *Almagest*. It was also
> shown that Galileo and Kepler rejected the Copernican
> Programme but accepted its Aristarchian hard core.
> Rather than *initiating* a revolution, Copernicus acted as

midwife to the birth of a programme of which he never dreamt, namely an anti-Ptolemaic program, which took astronomy *back* to Aristarchus and at the same time *forward* to a new dynamics. (p. 189).

The Copernican Revolution was progressive in its internal shift back to the Platonic heuristic. Lakatos wants to validate our intuition that the Copernican shift was a positive, scientific step, even though we now know that it was as wrong as the Ptolemaic system. Progressiveness in a tradition is not a matter of being correct. Also, to the extent that an internal shift is rational its reconstruction does not require sociological or psychological supports.

Lakatos stresses that he is not equating rationality with simplicity. He suggests that philosophers of science appeal to simplicity only because they realize that convention plays a role in theoretical decisions about conceptual change. Since philosophers quite correctly conclude that observations alone cannot determine which scheme or tradition is correct, they resort to a standard of overall simplicity. But Lakatos argues that "Simplicity seems to be relative to one's subjective taste" (p. 174) and therefore such a solution encourages relativism. Further, his study shows that when the revision of the hard core of Ptolemaic-Aristotelian astronomy occurred, simplicity followed automatically as an effect of, or as redefined as, preserving uniform circularity. When geocentrism was demoted to the status of a peripheral and thus modifiable claim (as against uniform circularity) then it also appeared as needlessly complicating the picture. But no bare criteria of simplicity demonstrates Copernicus's superiority. Rather, the tradition's superiority changes the standards of simplicity. Rational success precedes and determines aesthetic success.

Lakatos's appeal to historicity is therefore like Popper in that both ignore intention, feeling, or emotion in constructing the problem situation.

> Our account is a narrowly internalist one. No place in this account for the Renaissance spirit so dear to Kuhn's heart; for the turmoil of Reformation and Counter-reformation, no impact of the Churchman; no sign of any effect from the alleged or real rise of capitalism in the sixteenth century; no motivation from the needs of navigation so much cherished by Bernal. The whole development is narrowly

internal; its progressive part could have taken place at any time, given a Copernican genius, between Aristotle and Ptolemy or in any year after, say, the 1175 translation of the *Almagest* into Latin, or for that matter, by an Arab astronomer in the ninth century. External history *in this case* is not only secondary; it is nearly redundant. (pp. 188–89)

The methodology of research programs reconstructs what "should" or "could" have happened. It studies the possibility of rationality within a tradition. Historical narratives are quite simply "fabrications," Lakatos admits. But there are better or worse fabrications and when it comes to rationality there are "sharp criteria" of the best fabrications, namely those that make rationality internal. "The internal skeleton of rational history defines the external problems" (p. 191). Reconstruction is not a full historical account, only a full account of reason in history.

> Rational reconstruction (in the sense I use the term) cannot be comprehensive since human beings are not *completely* rational animals: and even when they act rationally they may have a false theory of their own rational actions. (p. 114).

Lakatos argues that theories of knowledge or methodology are implicitly theories of history. Thus, theories of knowledge can be tested (unlike trying to judge directly their methods for acquiring knowledge) by constructing histories on the basis of these standards and then "criticizing the rational historical reconstruction to which they lead" (p. 122). Lakatos came to this strategy of translating methodologies of science into historiographies of science after he tried and failed to criticize traditional methodologies on logical grounds. Lakatos concluded that all methodologies were sound and that there were always exceptions to any serious methodological rule. There appeared to be no way to criticize or reject any given methodological guideline. But by using the proposed methods as conjectures for historical reconstructions Lakatos thought he could "test" views of science. In comparing possible reconstructions, without relying on purely logical or epistemological grounds, the internal, explanatory "sweep" of the resulting histories could decide the issue.

From the argument that "all methodologies function as historio-graphical theories" some have interpreted Lakatos as offering a new, definitive methodology for science.[7] But Lakatos explicitly rejects the effort to find the "best" method for acquiring knowledge. Lakatos is arguing that the only criteria for making such a judgment is the "best" rational reconstruction of history of science.

> I soon had to discover that . . . my methodology too and any methodology whatsoever *can* be "falsified", for the simple reason that no set of human judgements is completely rational and thus no rational reconstruction can ever coincide with actual history.
>
> This recognition led me to propose a new *constructive* criterion by which methodologies *qua* rational reconstructions of history might be appraised. (p. 131)

Before discussing Lakatos' criterion of appraisal it is important to stress the concessions in this passage. Rational reconstruction does not exhaust historical complexity. In what was intended as a criticism of Lakatos, Feyerabend adapts a passage from Lenin to the effect that history will always be "richer in content, more varied, more many-sided, more lively and subtle than even the best historian and the best methodologist imagine."[8] But not only does Lakatos grant this point, he also concludes, like Feyerabend, that there can be no method of science: "science *is* rational, but its rationality cannot be subsumed under the general laws of any methodology" (p. 130). Lakatos gives no further reason to adopt the rubric of translating our theories of knowledge into historical interpretations. He does not explicitly entertain a Hegelian teleology in which the history of knowledge must culminate in our current standpoint. Lakatos's defense is simply the absence of any alternative standards in epistemology.

These historical rational reconstructions are always partial and forever incomplete because "rational reconstructions remain for-ever submerged in an ocean of anomalies" (p. 134). Therefore, Lakatos holds that instead of methodologies there can only be heuristic "rules of thumb" for how to proceed in inquiry. There is no "automatic" rationality because knowledge is always the product of traditions.

But how can such diverse historical narratives be appraised? How does Lakatos overcome the implicit relativism in, for example, Popper's realization that rationality depends on the problem situation faced by the theorist? Lakatos suggests that since a reconstruction intends to "recount" the history of science as rational, we judge narratives by how much the historical events become internally dictated by a pure methodological debate. Thus, a reconstruction with a rigid notion of rationality will produce only a slender amount of internal, rational history of science and a corresponding excess of external, supplementary, social history. Explanatory success is translating the dynamics of the tradition into matters of knowledge rather than culture.

> Each rational reconstruction produces some character-istic pattern of rational growth of scientific knowledge. But all these *normative* reconstructions may have to be supplemented by *empirical* external theories to explain the residual non-rational factors. The history of science is always richer than its rational reconstruction. (p. 118)

For Lakatos there is a constant "negotiation" along the boundary between internal and external reconstructive histories, one that depends on the sophistication of the method or theory of rationality. Lakatos's explicit guideline is that historical interpretations encompass as much as possible of the history of science into their picture of rationality and leave as little to psychological or sociological "epicycles." Thus, reconstructions have different "externalities." Lakatos judges a reconstruction on the breadth of its internal sweep and success. The less that anecdote and chronology and the more that theory of knowledge dictate reconstruction, the stronger and more sweeping the interpretation.

> Historiographical criticism frequently succeeds in destroying much of fashionable externalism. An "impressive", "sweeping", "far-reaching", external explanation is usually the hallmark of a weak methodological substructure; and, in turn, the hallmark of a relatively weak internal history (in terms of which most actual history is either inexplicable or anomalous) is that it leaves too much to be explained by external history. p. 134).

Criticism concerns the failure of a reconstruction to encompass enough of the historical events, as compared with alternative accounts. Criticism does not speak from some definitive account – since all reconstructions are provisional – but holds out a standard of internal sweep that allows us to choose between alternative historical accounts.

> Whatever problem the historian of science wishes to solve, he has first to reconstruct the relevant section of the growth of objective scientific knowledge, that is, the relevant section of "internal history". As it has been shown, what constitutes for him internal history depends on his philosophy, whether he is aware of this fact or not. (p. 118).

Lakatos has transformed epistemology into philosophy of history. Though this is reminiscent of Hegel (the philosopher Lakatos most dislikes) it differs from Hegelianism by assuming that there will be no final account. Also, by shifting to philosophy of history, Lakatos shifts the debate from the existence of competitive methodologies to whether or not there are comparative standards of rationality. Lakatos identifies "Wittgensteinians" – Stephen Toulmin for example – as "historicists" and "Hegelians" because they hold that the differences between "ways of life" or traditions cannot be judged. There are no universal standards, only diverse strategies. These new sceptics go too far, in Lakatos's view, in learning from fallibility and the failure of recipes for rationality. They abandon all hope for adjudicating between traditions and treat logic and reasoning as mere rhetorical persuasion. As with Popper, Lakatos wants to stand between dogmatism and relativism.

In a review of Stephen Toulin's *Human Understanding* Lakatos accuses Toulmin of reviving Hegelian historicism in philosophy of science.[9] Toulmin, according to Lakatos, reduces the philosopher of science to a social historian who can only describe or document that there have been standards for the production of knowledge in the past, but who cannot judge them. The historicist argument imprisons the thinker in the relativity of the present and leaves all intellectual battles as undecidable, cultural conflicts. When faced with conceptual conflicts historicism has no response. Lakatos concludes:

> Toulmin's answer is that in such cases where two or

more proposed "strategic redirections" are in conflict, only history will decide. Here he brings in the time-worn *ad hoc* strategem of historicism: the Long Run. . . . Toulmin, it seems, ought to hold that "true rationality" is revealed only in the "closed down long run," on the day of Final Judgement, when we are all dead.[10]

But can Lakatos really be such an uncompromising critic of this kind of historicism? Lakatos's own accounts of scientific progress, as has been shown, proceed by hindsight. He also admits that for the historical reconstruction of rationality "Of course, no statute law is either infallible or unequivocably interpretable."[11] Lakatos balances this admission with the promise that his appraisal of past methodologies has some "hard Popperian teeth."

> I inject some hard Popperian elements into the appraisal of whether a programme progresses or degenerates or of whether one is overtaking another. That is, I give criteria for progress and stagnation within a programme and also rules for the "elimination" of whole research programmes. A research programme is said to be progressing as long as its theoretical growth anticipates its empirical growth, that is, as long as it keeps predicting novel facts with some success (*"progressive problemshift"*); it is *stagnating* if its theoretical growth lags behind its empirical growth, that is, as long as it gives only *post hoc* explanations either of chance discoveries or of facts anticipated by, and discovered in, a rival programme (*"degenerating problemshift"*). (p. 112)

These criteria that balance against historicist relativism are neither surprising nor difficult to understand. Lakatos makes "success" rest on verifying the production of "excess content" in a program that cannot be falsified directly. Though no tradition can be knocked down by one piece of counterevidence it can be shown, "in the long run," to be either growing or degenerating. Of course, while recommending that a degenerating program be eliminated or shelved, Lakatos grants that working in such a tradition is not thereby irrational. As long as one explicitly recognizes the risk, it is rational to take chances.[12]

Since the rivalry between programs is a protracted and drawn out affair and since it is not clear that the Popperian "hard teeth" will result in any concrete decision, Lakatos appears to make normative judgments only in *hindsight*. Thus, like Toulmin, what Lakatos is putting forward is not some possible historical discovery or fact about the history of science, but a philosophy of history.

> In this methodology . . . there can be no instant – let alone mechanical – rationality. *Neither the logician's proof of inconsistency nor the experimental scientist's verdict of anomaly can defeat a research programme in one blow.* One can be "wise" only after the event. . . . There is never anything inevitable about the triumph of a programme. Also there is never anything inevitable about its defeat. (p. 113)

Has Lakatos provided anything more here than the retrospective historicism he attacks in Toulmin? Lakatos's approach claims that there are universal standards of growth but that these can only be applied as historical reconstructions of the past. If we use them in the present we would kill potentially promising traditions. But Lakatos has taken a theoretically laborious way of saying the obvious. Historians who take the present state of knowledge as their reference point can "reconstruct" the history of science as a pattern of growth and degeneration. What concerns Toulmin is that if the present changes, then the reconstruction changes and our so-called "solutions" to historical problems are revealed as ideological – that is, reflecting an historical prejudice or bias. Lakatos, like the early Popper, both admits the role of interest and perspective in history but simply refuses to see any special philosophical problem in that admission.

Perhaps the problem with Lakatos's position can be brought out if I return once more to the Copernican example. While most people believe intuitively that the Copernican Revolution was a genuinely scientific, progressive, and rational change, Lakatos wants to demonstrate that belief objectively. What could constitute such a demonstration? Copernicanism must have generated – whether that was known to its adherents or not – excess content, predicted novel facts over its competitors, and predicted known facts in a "novel," that is, less ad hoc, fashion than did its competitors. These are the criteria of a progressive problemshift. All we need are these internal factors to baptise this change as rational.

The novel facts predicted by Copernicanism were the phases of Venus and stellar parallax. Lakatos does, however, quickly qualify that claim. He admits an anomaly in his reconstruction. Recall that Lakatos is attempting to demonstrate that Copernicanism was progressive and rational without appealing to external cultural factors or psychological factors about what persons did or did not believe at that time. He has no patience for arguments about the enthusiasm of young people for new ideas and the general influence of the Italian Renaissance on these same minds. But the predicted novel fact of the phases of Venus was not corroborated until 1616, with Galileo's telescope. Even if evidence of Galileo's observation was taken at face value, Lakatos also argues that by 1616 Copernicanism was already obsolete and being abandoned for a "new dynamic-oriented physics." Thus the novel fact or confirmed excess content marks not the point at which it was rational to accept Copernicanism, but the point at which to abandon it. Again, the best that can be said is that even from this event it is only in hindsight that Copernicanism was rational.

The second novel fact, stellar parallax, is similarly problematic. The Copernican system, since it moves the earth, implies that in sighting stars there should be an apparent "shift," because the stars are being sighted from a body moving in a large orbit. Detecting shifts in the position of stars due to the movement of the earth requires measuring extremely small angles and demands exacting and laborious work. Corrections have to be made according to the motion of the stars and the refraction of the atmosphere. The vast majority of stars do not have detectable parallaxes and the method can only be used for stars within 300 light years. For all these reasons stellar parallax was not confirmed until the 1830s and by then in a wholly different research program. How can that distant confirmation, far in the future and in the context of radically different debates, have made Copernicanism more rational than its competitors in the past?

We can understand Lakatos's distaste for hindsight. In both of these cases historical hindsight seems arbitrary in what confirmations it picks out as significant; it seems to rest upon, rather than explain, our original "intuition" about the rationality of theories. Lakatos thus suggests one more criteria. He suggests that

Copernicus explained "known facts" in a "dramatic" and less ad hoc manner. Lakatos stresses the often made point that the movement of the planets appeared more "natural" and regular once the earth moved. Copernicus's distinction, for example, between planets "inferior to" the earth (between the earth and the sun) and "superior to" the earth (beyond the earth's orbit) suddenly made movements that were complex and anomalous in the Ptolemaic system completely simple and clear. For example, Copernicanism easily explained the observation that Venus and Mercury never "elongated" very far from the sun.

Thus the "facts" concerning planetary motion – though known to both systems – were explained more "straightforwardly" by Copernicus, and that supports the intuition that the system was more rational and progressive. This argument, however, sounds a great deal like a traditional defense of the criteria of simplicity that Lakatos rejects for its relativism. In fact, Lakatos said that it was the internal rationality of change that produced as an effect the "feeling" that one system was simpler than another. Here Lakatos's whole account appears dangerously circular.

But even ignoring what seems a return to conventionalism by Lakatos, the argument is much weaker than Lakatos claims. He says: "But all research programmes I admire have one characteristic in common. They all predict novel facts, facts which had been either undreamt of, or have indeed been contradicted by previous or rival programmes" (p. 5). That stronger claim, as we saw, fails to account for Copernicus's superiority on internal rational grounds. On Lakatos's own account the suggested modification is not strong enough because Lakatos explicitly treats "ad hoc" strategies as historical. That point is essential to Lakatos's demand for patience and no "quick kill." If Copernicus could appeal to his more "natural" account of planetary behavior to show that his shift was rational, then the Ptolemaic-Aristotelians could, and did, appeal to the "naturalness" of the stable earth for explaining the behavior of moving bodies on earth. We are back to a Kuhnian stand off between traditions and, consequently, the call for an "external" account to resolve the question.

Without ever discussing it explicitly in his writings, Lakatos appears to use at lest two conceptions of rationality. One is historicist and is reflected in his Hegelian appeal to "hindsight."

For example, he says; *"It is not only the ('internal') success or the ('internal') defeat of a programme which can be judged only with hindsight: it is frequently also its content"* (p. 119). Rationality here is the radically improved history which is only possible because of where we are now, in the present. It is this rationality which demands that:

> One must treat budding programmes leniently; pro-
> grammes may take decades before they get off the ground
> and become empirically progressive. Criticism is not a
> Popperian quick kill, by refutation. Important criticism
> is always constructive: there is no refutation without a
> better theory. (p. 6)

This charitable and lenient rationality is at odds with Lakatos's second conception of rationality which might be called universal and prescriptive. The second conception contains Popperian "hard teeth" and definitive standards. The issue is not that Lakatos distorts the "real" events in the case studies but that he wavers between a historicist "understanding" of a program and a hard-line decision procedure for progress in knowledge.

As Lakatos's critics have been anxious to point out, there seems to be a vicious circularity here.[13] Lakatos sets up rational reconstructions by constituting the research program. In this way, the advantage of hindsight comes into the definition of the standards which will then be "tested" in history. By knowing who the "winners" and "losers" are Lakatos can already build into the ideal research program, and the externalities he will exclude, the very progress his methodology claims to demonstrate. In practice Lakatos's methodology will never err because it will always replicate the current assessment of what is or is not rational. His two conceptions of rationality always converge in the present. Lakatos's judgment about whether an event is a momentary degeneration or a long-term decline into irrationality or pseudo-science is not supplied by Lakatos's reconstruction, but simply by already knowing the out-come in distant historical cases or being circumspect in judgments about current disputes.

Lakatos's approach is fundamentally retrospective and in that sense fundamentally historicist. Lakatos, of course, condemns historicism because it is, in his view, a wholly descriptive study of history which relativizes all standards. Lakatos is quite right to condemn the effort at a wholly descriptive history. Such a "view from nowhere" would not be a history at all, if it can even be imagined. But historicism more specifically argues that the viewpoints from which history can be reconstructed vary and are as multiple as the interests and prejudgments that make up the rational decisions within any given context. A totally normative history, however, turns out to be just as shallow as the descriptivist dream. What Lakatos sees as his normative judgments about the history of theory turn out to be cultural opinions resting on what is "obvious" in the present and the lack of any defensible alternative assumptions. Thus, there is a dogmatic strain in Lakatos that emerges, for example, when he takes Toulmin to task for allowing that perhaps all rational reconstructions are provisional and open to change. Toulmin rightly expresses surprise at how ideas which he believes are inherent in Lakatos's approach are treated by Lakatos as not merely wrong but positively immoral and dangerous when expressed by others.[14]

Lakatos's view is historical to the extent that he emphasizes how protocols and procedures of research are conventional and heuristic. But that minimal sense of historicity would result in a classical relativism without Lakatos's simultaneous assertion that there are universal criteria for appraising these heuristics. But criteria, even if they do exist as stated by Lakatos, are not the *result* of historical studies of science. His case studies, as he willingly admits, are "shaped" and therefore exemplify already arrived at normative conclusions. If Lakatos's norms – which he often simply alludes to without an argument – are based on present knowledge projected into the past then his argument is historicist. In a recent work, Ian Hacking raises, from a different perspective, a similar concern about Lakatos's approach.

> Lakatos's histories are normative in that he can conclude that a given chunk of research "ought not to have" gone the way it did, and that it went that way through the interference of external factors not germane to the programme. In concluding that a chosen case was not "rational" it is permissible to go against current scientific wisdom. But although in principle Lakatos can countenance this, he is properly moved by respect for the implicit appraisals of working scientists. I cannot see Lakatos

willingly conceding that Einstein, Bohr, Lavoisier or even Copernicus was participating in an irrational programme . . . Rationality will simply be defined by what a present community calls good, and nothing shall counterbalance the extraterrestrial weight of an Einstein.[15]

The problem is not only Lakatos's respect for scientists but a balance between the claims about universal principles of progress and a reflection of our current, and therefore provisional, assessment of scientific history. Historicists are "perspectivists" because they reject the existence of a single "plot" or vantage point for history. The authority of the present then provides only one possible solution, and an historically relative solution. It rejects alternatives that do not share in the "obviousness" of our present sense of historical teleology.

For example, in *Representing and Intervening*, Hacking reviews the history of what physicists call "the Michelson-Morely experiment" and juxtaposes Hacking's "experimentalist version" of the events against Lakatos's reconstruction. Hacking claims Lakatos distorts and misinterprets the "actual" events in an effort to fit his methodological guidelines.

Lakatos writes: "Michelson first devised an experiment in order to test Fresnel's and Stokes' contradictory theories about the influence of the motion of the earth on the aether."

That is not true, As experimenter Michelson wanted to do what Maxwell said was impossible, namely measure the motion of the earth relative to the aether. . . . He says just that in a letter to Simon Newcomb, dated Berlin, 22 November, 1880.

Lakatos writes: "Michelson's long series of experiments from 1881 to 1935, conducted in order to test subsequent versions of the aether program, provides a fascinating example of a degenerating problem shift." Well, the experiments he did from 1931 to 1935 must be on the astral plane, for he died in 1931.[16]

Earlier in the book, oddly enough, Hacking defended Lakatos's free-wheeling rational reconstructions. "Just as in any other inquiry, there is nothing wrong with trying to re-analyze the data. That does not mean lying. It may mean simply reconsidering or selecting and arranging the facts, or it may be a case of imposing a new research programme on the known historical facts."[17]

In spite of Hacking's reasonable defense of reconsidering and selecting historical data, Hacking's own alternative interpretation or "reading" of the Michelson-Morley case, namely the experimentalist account, highlights the problem. Rational reconstructions are possible without resolving the question of which account is correct. In that sense, Lakatos is not "whiggish" because he does not take contemporary science as definitive. What Lakatos claims is that the intellectual decisions that shaped the present are rational. In arguing with Lakatos, Hacking appeals to what Michelson wrote and to the date he died, and – contrary to his own defense of rational recon- struction – assumes these are decisive "known historical facts." It is precisely these kinds of facts that are dismissed by Lakatos as "external" and open to free-play in rational reconstruction. What Hacking has shown is that rational reconstruction cannot literally "test" a theory of history. Thus Hacking concludes:

> There are many more published fantasies about the Michelson-Morley experiment, and I certainly do not claim finality for my brief sketch. I chose Lakatos for an object lesson because I think his own philosophy is important. However, when it comes to drawing theoretical inferences from real-life cases, as with Prout or Michelson, the inference is always much too speedy. A theory-dominated philosophy blinds one to reality.[18]

The problem lies deeper. Lakatos is "speedy" in his interpre- tation, playing freely with historical documentation, because the theoretical object guiding the inquiry, the research program, is a prescriptive standard. The aim is not description. Further, if Hacking suggests another pattern to impose (thereby selecting other facts) it serves another reconstruction or interpretation – the story of experimentalism, not reality itself. Lakatos gladly admits that "what happened" in history is constructed. Thus Hacking's accusation that Lakatos's histories are "potted" is true, but, to Lakatos, the invented character of his histories is not the issue. For Lakatos, there are no non-potted narratives.

I agree with Hacking's dissatisfaction with Lakatos, but not because of the priority of experimentation over theory, or the priority of historical data over rational reconstruction. I think the problem in Lakatos is precisely in his account of historical interpretation. The problem can be seen in Lakatos's version of the Copernican revolution when he admits that the distinction between hard core and heuristic is arbitrary.

> Both *programmes* [Ptolemy and Copernicus] branched off from the Pythagorean-Platonic programme whose basic principle was that since heavenly bodies are perfect, all astronomical phenomena should be saved by a combination of as few uniform circular motions (or uniform spherical rotations about an axis) as possible. This principle remained the cornerstone of the heuristic of both programmes. This proto-programme contained no directives as to where the center of the universe lies. The heuristic in this case was primary, the "hard core" secondary. (pp. 180-81).

In a significant footnote to this passage Lakatos adds that the distinction between hard core and heuristic "is frequently a matter of convention." That admission brings to the surface the indeterminacy and circularity of rational reconstruction. If the fundamental distinction in his interpretive methodology is arbitrary or conventional, then its version of history is no more than a strategy within a tradition or culture. The notions of degeneracy and progressiveness themselves reflect traditions. To convert them into universal judgments about history rests, then, on a *decision* – namely on the distinction between hard core and heuristic. But that decision is internal to a tradition, embedded in a program. All Lakatos has shown is that those histories in conformity with our present knowledge will *appear* more rational. Thus, as Paul Feyerabend argues, Lakatos's vast methodological machinery is simply rhetorical persuasion.

> Now we have seen that the particular standards which Lakatos has chosen neither issue abstract orders (such as "eliminate theories that are inconsistent with accepted basic statements") nor do they contain general judgements

concerning the rationality or irrationality of a course of action (such as "it is irrational to stick to a theory that contradicts accepted basic statements"). Such orders and judgements have given way to *concrete decisions in complex historical situations.* [emphasis added]. . . . It puts teeth into the standards not by strengthening their power in argument, but by creating a historical situation in which it becomes very difficult, *practically*, to pursue a degenerating research programme.[19]

Lakatos admits a conventional aspect of his accounts of progress but ignores the clash between that admission and his promise of *universal* criteria with "bite." As Hacking so nicely puts it, we no longer "show our respect for science by dehistoricizing it"[20] and perhaps Lakatos is the last stand against how historicist we have become.

5

Historical A Priori

While Lakatos explores the internal rationality of tradition through its historical reconstruction, he also holds to certain normative standards that would make such a reconstruction unnecessary. If he can stipulate what makes knowledge rational then that it not the part of knowledge which is historical, and vice versa. This difficulty appears in Lakatos's paraphrase of Kant to the effect that history of science without philosophy of science is blind and philosophy of science without the history of science is empty. The statement suggests a relationship of history and knowledge that raises relativist concerns, concerns that both Lakatos and Popper find disconcerting.

Another way of posing the question is to ask whether histories of knowledge can dispense with already assuming a fixed meaning for rationality. Can our present standards be bracketed or suspended? In trying to assess the implications of such questions I have chosen a writer whom critics consistently accuse of encouraging an extreme historical and cultural relativism. For example, Hilary Putnam claims that Michel Foucault historicizes the activity of reason in his work and thus treats everything from the study of diseases to criminology as ideological. He suggests that Foucault "is trying to show us how every culture lives, thinks, sees, makes love, by a set of unconscious guiding assumptions with non-rational determinants. If previous ideologies now seem 'irrational' it is because we judge them by our culture-bond notion of rationality."[1]

Foucault ends up, in Putnam's view, with no objective position from which to judge past disputes. Putnam is perplexed, however, by the fact that Foucault nevertheless claims a "mysterious standpoint and even objectivity in some of his works."[2]

In the discussion that follows I will draw selectively on Foucault's work as it relates to the problems of historicism and relativism rather than summarize his various books.[3] Foucault's historical studies are a way to do theory of knowledge. In this context, Putnam would agree, I suspect, that Foucault is not an historicist in Popper's original sense of the term. That is, Foucault does not appeal to a logic, order, or meaning to history. He explicitly rejects teleological accounts of history and the search for historical laws. He calls Marxism a "battle in a children's wading pool" and, like Popper, rejects a single historical "plot." In *The Order of Things* Foucault challenges the traditional history of ideas that reconstructs the past only from current knowledge. "Historians want to write histories of biology in the 19th century, but they do not realize that biology did not exist then, and that the pattern of knowledge which has been familiar to us for a hundred and fifty years is not valid for a previous period."[4] Different reconstructions are possible.

Putnam calls *The Birth of the Clinic* Foucault's best example of such an alternative history, an inventive story of how the "clinical experience" in modern medicine was constructed. Foucault recounts through the history of medicine how a specific "way of seeing," neither natural nor necessary, was institutionalized, justified, and made to seem natural: "There have been, and will be, other distributions of illness."[5] Histories of medicine traditionally suppress the possibility of any other distribution by portraying modern medicine as the triumph of empiricism and experimentation over speculation.

Foucault's work is built as an attack on traditional histories and such epistemological assumptions as the separation between observations and language. Clinical experience in the history of medicine is usually treated as direct contact with reality "prior to all discourse." But, for Foucault, the clinical experience is a systematic reorganization of knowledge, rather than what naturally results after superstitious beliefs have been abandoned. It is, as Foucault calls it, a specific "gaze" meant to reveal a manifest truth.

"Medicine made its appearance as a clinical science in conditions which define, together with its historical possibility, the domain of its experience and the structure of its rationality" (p. xv).

Foucault begins the book with a clash between two "reports" about membranous tissues. The first by Pierre Pomme (1769) is a "language of fantasy" concerning intestine which peel off their "internal tunics, which we saw emerge from the rectum." This report lacks a "perceptual base" *for us* claims Foucault. He contrasts it with a "normal" report from Gaspard-Laurent Bayle (1825) concerning a brain lesion and the "false membranes" often found on patients with chronic meningitis.

These two incompatible reports of "what was seen" are the result of deep epistemological shifts. Pomme is not irrational, confused, hallucinatory, or reporting rumor and dogma as though it were fact. Rather, Foucault suggests that Pomme "sees" what he describes, but that his qualitative language and imagery externalize what is now relegated to the subjective feelings and impressions of illness. Pomme's world does not separate things and words or primary and secondary qualities, as would later seem natural. With Pomme, "language and its object are one." Foucault thus asks the typical historicist question: "How can we be sure than an eighteenth-century doctor did not see what he saw, but that it needed several decades before the fantastic figures were dissipated to reveal, in the space they vacated the shape of things as they really are?" (p. x).

Foucault makes a case for a link between the teleological histories of knowledge, in which observation triumphs over superstition, and a philosophical position that truth manifests itself to sight. The history of medicine in which irrational myths are slowly replaced by empirical inquiry is sustained by the assumption of an "unconceptualized confrontation of a gaze." These histories are intended to teach a lesson. The narrative reinforces what appears in the present as obvious, natural, or normal. Traditional histories rest on the search for a neutral semantic or syntactic sign that marks an account as rational, that distinguishes real from fictitious explanation.

Putnam argues that Foucault's consequent scepticism about rational standards ends up eating away at his own claims. But Foucault's alternative histories could be taken as merely raising doubts and questions about the assumptions behind histories of knowledge. He questions whether there can be an account of reason independent of these different historical reconstructions. Whether that position commits Foucault to irrationalism is a separate question. It does lead Foucault to reject certain traditional semantic signs of objectivity. For example, the absence of metaphors in a discourse is not necessarily a marker of its scientific status. Conditions for objectivity in description are historical and thus the line between metaphor and recording shifts.

> What sharp line divides a description that depicts membranes as being like "damp parchment" from that other equally qualitative, equally metaphorical description of them laid out over the tunic of the brain, like a film of egg whites? Do Bayle's "white" and "red" membranes possess greater value, solidity and objectivity – in terms of scientific discourse – than the horny scales described by the doctors of the eighteenth century? (p.xi)

Foucault is not concerned with documenting what Pomme, for example, did or did not believe, but with the theoretical context which made Pomme's statements possible. Foucault's histories are philosophical and often eschew what was actually said or intended for a formal analysis of theoretical statements. Thus Foucault's views about language and culture are more complex than the simple cultural or sociological relativism Putnam finds. Foucault studies how "things," rather than manifesting themselves to the innocent eye, are "systematized from the outset, thus making them thereafter endlessly accessible to new discourses and open to the task of transforming them" (p. xix).

Because there will be and have been other "distributions of illness," Foucault attaches no privilege to the current classifications and concepts of illness. Thus an historical relativism emerges when Foucault argues:

> The exact superposition of the "body" of the disease and the body of the sick man is no more than a historical, temporary datum. Their encounter is self-evident only for us, or rather, we are only just beginning to detach ourselves from it. (p. 3).

Inside the historical present concepts appear self-evident.

Foucault hints at a Hegelian theme that we only become self-conscious of such assumptions as they pass away, as we look back. The term "gaze" (*le regard*), which recurs throughout the book, refers then to a "natural attitude" toward the world. The gaze conceals that its experience is constructed, that perception and conception are already synthesized. Thus studies of the gaze as a form of perception are always retrospective and historical. In its historical moment the gaze is the natural attitude, the "innocent eye" revealing the world as it really is.

Foucault throughout his book organizes the discussion around a distinction between classificatory and clinical approaches to disease. In classification – which dominates what Foucault calls the Classical Age – he detects a framework in which diseases are autonomous entities, having natural histories and ideal forms that are distorted by the patient's body. Patients and doctors are both, in this model, disturbances. Therefore, classification depends on a specific notion of observation which, for example, does not expect that a disease can be *seen* in its effects. Under this Classicism a "qualitative gaze" emerged, as in Pomme's fantastic imagery. Pomme's language is possible because that is how Classical representation allows for the manifestation of disease.

During the period in which medicine was dominated by classification, therefore, there are no case histories: "If one wishes to know the illness from which he is suffering, one must subtract the individual, with his particular qualities" (p. 14). Foucault stresses, however, that this pre-modern discourse about disease was a coherent and *rational* practice which linked disease with "successful" areas of knowledge such as botany. But classificatory medicine does not produce the clinical experience, the hospital, the dossier, or the cure as those terms or practices are now understood. Rather this specific classificatory model, which Foucault calls "the medicine of species," privileges a different set of "spaces."

> The natural locus of disease is the natural locus of life –
> the family: gentle, spontaneous care, expressive love and
> a common desire for a cure, assists nature in its struggle
> against the illness, and allows the illness itself to attain its
> own truth. The hospital doctor sees only distorted, altered
> diseases, a whole teratology of the pathological; . . . The

medicine of species implies therefore a free spatialization for the disease, with no privileged region, no constraint imposed by hospital conditions –. . . . It [disease] must not be fixed in a medically prepared domain, but be allowed . . . to "vegetate" in its original soil: the family, a social space conceived in its most natural, most primitive, most morally secure form, both enclosed upon itself and entirely transparent, where illness is left to itself. (pp. 17–18).

Foucault's point is that the scheme behind the "medicine of species" is a defensible, rational approach which made possible certain social practices, emphasizing family assistance, the home, and the "collective space." In what Lakatos would call an internal history, Foucault makes the political or economic dimension of health depend on a discourse of knowledge. Those social practices ultimately rest on theoretical decisions. For Foucault, cultural institutions like the clinic reflect epistemological strategies. The new institutional "spaces" for disease in the clinics and hospitals, the "spaces" replacing the family, are *first* explained internally as an epistemic shift. The economic and institutional change is brought within the sweep of Foucault's conceptual history. The history of systems of knowledge explains how and why institutions and social practices change. Thus if Foucault is a relativist he is not a traditional cultural relativist.

Though *The Birth of the Clinic* is far from an ordinary history of medicine Foucault does bring in the classic theme of how epidemics and contagion transformed medicine. The difference is that in Foucault's treatment the older classificatory medicine is not treated as incapable of understanding or practically responding to plagues. Classificatory medicine could conceptualize contagion, but not an infectious agent. "The basis of this perception is not a specific type, but a nucleus of circumstances. The basis of an epidemic is not pestilence or catarrh: it is Marseilles in 1721. . . . The essential basis is determined by the time, the place" (p. 23).

The standard histories of medicine argue that epidemics and the failure to control their spread brought down a previous age's medical follies. In contrast Foucault emphasizes how *both* classificatory and clinical medicine sought, while conceptually distinct, "information, supervision and constraint." Both were rational. The difference was that clinical medicine sought causal explanations whereas the classificatory model looked for "a homogeneous surface in which analogies can be read."

> Each day Razoux made meterological and climatic observations, which he then compared with a nosological analysis of patients under observation and with the evolution, crises, and outcome of the diseases. A system of coincidences then appeared that indicated a causal connexion and also suggested kinships or new links between diseases. (pp. 29–30).

Such medical inquiry would not produce clinical solutions but it still "supervised" health and studied the frequency of births and deaths. Clinical medicine did not fully emerge until the nineteenth century, and Foucault attempts to show in his book that the "fantastic" medicine of analogies, spaces, and classifications which preceded it was not refuted by empirical knowledge and was a rational practice capable of progress.

Foucault puts a twist on the familiar story of how "causal analysis" emerged. Foucault agrees that a shift occurred from "the demarcation of a surface in which analogies can be read" (the old classificatory medicine) to the "attribution of causality" (the new medicine). Other medical historians agree about the importance of this epistemological shift.[6] But Foucault concludes that, therefore, the act of perception itself cannot be decisive in the history of medicine because it is precisely the result, both in institutions and theories, rather than the cause of such changes. "What now constituted the unity of the medical gaze . . . was not the perception of the patient in his singularity but a collective consciousness, with all the information that intersects in it, growing in a complex, ever-proliferating way until it finally achieves the dimensions of a history, a geography, a state" (p. 29).

In a central chapter, "The Lessons of the Hospital," Foucault presents hospitals as not only places for treatment but as pedagogic institutions whose purpose is to train for the clinical gaze, a "childhood gaze" as Foucault calls it. "The discourse of the world passes through open eyes, eyes open at every instant as for the first time" (p. 65). The hospital as a school rests on the premise that "truth teaches itself." Thus the "birth of the clinic" as an institution was preceded by the birth of an epistemic possibility, the innocent eye. The clinic or hospital created an "observer" who was not only linked to a new conception of knowledge, but in turn generated new social utilities and a myth of "political purity." The innocent eye is the myth of modern medicine's emergence.

> [W]hat occurred was the restructuring, in a precise historical context, of the theme of "medicine in liberty": in liberated domain, the necessity of the truth that communicated itself to the gaze was to define its own institutional and scientific structure. . . . What hitherto had been lacking, "the very practice of the art, the observation of patients in their beds", was to become the essential part of the new medicine. (p. 69).

Foucault considers these "silent" epistemological shifts and the pedagogy that accompanies them as raising political and moral questions. As patients become objects for observation the clinic raises the question as to whether the poor should be required to be "the object of the gaze" just because they must go to a clinic. Foucault sees in his historically constructed objectivity "a tacit form of violence" and a mirror of the "terms of the contract" in the clinic.

> But to look in order to know, to show in order to teach, is not this a tacit form of violence, all the more abusive for its silence, upon a sick body that demands to be comforted, not displayed? Can pain be a spectacle? . . . Since disease can be cured only if others intervene with their knowledge, their resources, . . . illnesses of some should be transformed into the experience of others; and that pain should be enabled to manifest itself: . . .
>
> These then were the terms of the contract by which rich and poor participated in the organization of clinical experience. . . . The hospital became viable for private initiative from the moment that sickness, which had come to seek a cure, was turned into a spectacle. (pp. 84–85).

Knowledge requires a "deep structure of visibility." Ways of seeing and investigating make possible practices and institutions. The hospital was born not of an inevitable or natural necessity but out of a set of practices resulting from the clinical gaze; namely the internal demand for control, systematic observation, collections of cases and patient histories. The family or natural place in which disease manifests its essence disappear. The home suddenly becomes an uncontrolled domain where diseases are disturbed, obscured, and, most important, not compared with other cases. "As soon as medical knowledge is defined in terms of frequency, one no longer needs a natural environment; what one needs is a neutral domain, one that is homogeneous in all its parts and in which comparison is possible and open to any form of pathological event, with no principle of selection or exclusion" (p. 109).

Foucault's particular version of medical history is of interest because, like Conant and Kuhn, he tries to reveal a rationality internal to alien traditions, practices, and conceptual schemes. Also, in reconstructing the clinical experience Foucault reminds us of how what is habitual in the present seems natural; how common sense conceals interpretation by identifying itself as direct contact with the object. The clinic's success as a medical practice is an historical event in the continuing relationship between the body and disease. In the clinic's pedagogy, truth was always there in the past to be seen if only the blinders of prejudice, bad theory, and "hearsay" could be removed. History is a kind of erosion of error. "Thus this sensory knowledge – which nevertheless implies the conjunction of a hospital domain and a pedagogic domain, the definition of a field of probability and linguistic structure of the real – is reduced to praise of the immediate sensibility" (p. 121).

But Foucault's history is not simply a description of those events surrounding the "birth" of the clinic. If Foucault has written a history, it is, curiously, not a narrative of what happened in the history of medicine. It is more a critical commentary on traditional histories through a hypothetical reconstruction of the concepts behind medical thinking and the connection between concepts and institutional practices. It is not a history of what past figures actually said, did, or wrote, but the framework behind statements – a framework or schema neither expressible nor conscious in the past while embodied in the practices of the past. As an example of his approach, Foucault objects to the traditional account of why there was opposition to autopsies.

> For a hundred and fifty years, the same explanation
> had been repeated: medicine could gain access to that
> which founded it scientifically only by circumventing,
> slowly and prudently, one major obstacle, the opposition
> of religion, morality, and stubborn prejudice to the opening
> up of corpses. Pathological anatomy had had no more than
> a shadowy existence, on the edge of prohibition, . . . With
> the coming of the Enlightenment, death too was entitled to
> the clear light of reason and became, for the philosophical
> mind, an object and source of knowledge. (p. 124–25)

Foucault rejects this familiar story because it requires discrete
but important theoretical decisions. It paints a picture of progress
in observation, faithfulness to sense data, the rejection of theory for
experiment, the manifest theory of truth, and, finally, an eternal,
given relationship between subject and object in knowledge. Traditional history of ideas wants to privilege this new description of the
body. Foucault, on the contrary, is interested in what cannot be seen
in the body, namely that which makes it possible as a document.

> The access of the medical gaze into the sick body was
> not the continuation of a movement of approach that had
> been developing in a more or less regular fashion since
> the day when the first doctor cast his somewhat unskilled
> gaze from afar on the body of the first patient: it was the
> result of a recasting at the level of epistemic knowledge
> (*savoir*) itself, and not at the level of accumulated, refined,
> deepened, adjusted knowledge (*connaissances*). (p. 137)

The demand to "open a few corpses" was not a simple, empirical
requirement blocked superstitiously by religious authorities. It was a
very precise theoretical demand and was only possible as a practice
within a new framework of disease. Autopsy was not the result of
an accumulation of evidence. In Foucault's account, for example,
the classificatory or spatial models held that the essential nature of
disease could only be revealed if diseases were separated from the
specifics of the patient's body. Death was thus an event separable
from disease and not a part of the disease's natural history. The disease was an autonomous entity such that "if the traces of the disease

happened to bite into the corpse, then no evidence could distinguish absolutely between what belonged to it and what to death: their signs intersected in indecipherable disorder" (pp. 140–41). In the framework of a classificatory, "botany" of disease there were good theoretical reasons why a corpse could tell nothing about the nature of disease and why dissecting corpses would actually obscure the signs of disease and thus knowledge about it.

But later it was suddenly possible to think that a "disease is an autopsy . . . of the body, dissection alive." How did that change occur? As I have argued, Foucault's approach is not external, by which I mean he does not shift to a sociological, ideological (concerning religion or morality), or institutional account for these changes in knowledge. The practice of autopsy was not a cultural breakthrough. Rather it was a practice possible because the "field of the visible" changed. Thus the opposition to autopsy was not prejudiced or irrational. To recognize the utility of such a practice, and to accept the institutions that must accompany it, required an entirely new set of assumptions, arguments, concepts, and strategies of reasoning. But this entire new strategy could not be directly argued for or defended, it came about in fragments.

> This conceptual mastery of death was first acquired, at a very elementary level, by the organization of clinics. The possibility of opening up corpses immediately, thus reducing to a minimum the latency period between death and the autopsy, made it possible for the last stage of pathological time and the first stage of cadaveric time almost to coincide. The effects of organic decomposition were virtually suppressed, . . . so the moment of death may act as a marker . . . as the scalpel does organic space. (p. 141)

Foucault's story is about how dead bodies could become laboratories for the study and cure of living bodies, how "looking" at a patient could be taught, constructed, and institutionalized, and how reasoning about even death and disease is historically transitory.

In considering the implications of Foucault's historical approach to knowledge, *The Birth of the Clinic* needs to be amplified by passages from Foucault's *The Order of Things* where he specifically discusses historicism and relativism. I will weave through Foucault's discussion of historicism the work of the philosopher of science, Larry Laudan. Laudan criticizes traditional history of ideas in ways similar to Foucault, though he resolves the problem of relativism in a quite different fashion.

Whenever Foucault discusses what he is doing he begins by rejecting traditional history. In *The Order of Things*, Foucault explores similarities across three different historical periods between studies of language, economics, and biology. But even my summary is misleading since Foucault does not want to take our current disciplinary conception of linguistics, economics, or biology as fixed. Traditional intellectual history immediately seizes on a conflict between reason and superstition, or science and theology, looking for signs in past knowledge of a groping toward future scientific breakthroughs.

Larry Laudan's *Progress and Its Problems* also questions the assumptions behind history of ideas. Laudan agrees that theories must be understood as more than groups of logically connected statements. Theories are solutions to historical problem situations and the precise point of a historical reconstruction is to reveal the context for inquiry and reasoning. Laudan points out that in traditional history of ideas problems are assumed to be eternal and thus treated, for example, as "*the* problem of substance" or "*the* mind-body problem." "To *assume* problem identity through time is, for the historian of ideas, the first step on the road to what may be a most serious falsification of the historical record, for when we misconceive the precise character of a thinker's problems, we are apt to misunderstand the nature of the solutions he proposes."[7]

In *The Order of Things* Foucault also stresses the consequences of this presupposition or bias toward "identity" in traditional history of ideas. These consequences are part of a retrospective reading in which the present is projected into the past as a common experience. This method leads to a systematic blindness. Its assumption of identity, for example, may lead historical inquiry to *not see* connections between very different procedures such as, according to Foucault, taxonomic classification and microscopic observation. Further, the assumption is made that when recording data or facts one can always distinguish the experimentalists from the theorists or system builders. Finally, the overall history is ruled by conceptions of what is already known (under such notions as inheritance and influence) from what is yet to be discovered (under notions of anticipation or prophecy). These tools of intellectual history are all suspect. Foucault challenges "above all the application of categories that are strictly anachronistic in relation to this knowledge. . . . Historians . . . do not realize that . . . the pattern of knowledge that has been familiar to us . . . is not valid for a previous period."[8]

Foucault holds, for example, that this bias in the history of ideas toward continuity and teleology has falsified the importance of whole periods that do not fit our expectations, such as the Classical Age. Particular methods, such as natural history or classification by tables, are only treated as they anticipate some later science. As can be seen from Foucault's history of medicine, he is fascinated with knowledge systematized through the tables, classifications, and orders of the Classical Age – that period separating the Renaissance from modernism. In Foucault's account, natural histories were not meticulous examinations of evidence preparing for modern scientific research. The model of a natural history is an historically specific way to see and describe things, another language ordering and making knowledge possible. Classicism was not preparation for the triumph of observation over speculation, nor was it a necessary step toward modern natural sciences after centuries of superstitious blindness. In fact it was a point at which what was visible *shrank*, becoming restricted, regulated, and conceptualized in a rigid way.

> Natural history did not become possible because men looked harder and more closely. One might say, strictly speaking, that the Classical age used its ingenuity, if not to see as little as possible, at least to restrict deliberately the area of its experience. Observation, from the seventeenth century onward, is a perceptible knowledge furnished with a series of systematically negative conditions. Hearsay is excluded, that goes without saying; but so are taste and smell, because their lack of certainty and their variability render impossible any analysis into distinct elements that could be universally acceptable. . . . The area of visibility in which observation is able to assume its powers is thus only what is left after these exclusions: a visibility freed from all other sensory burdens and

restricted, moreover, to black and white. (pp. 132–33).

Seeing is selective and prepared; reading how the world can be represented must be learned. In the seventeenth and eighteenth centuries a "visible space" was constructed in classical representation that made botany or classification fruitful and significant. As a result of these procedures, there were parallel social practices and institutions which transformed the activities of gathering knowledge, observing the world, and collecting information.

> At the institutional level, the inevitable correlatives of this patterning were botanical gardens and natural history collections. And their importance, for Classical culture, does not lie essentially in what they make it possible to see, but in what they hide and in what, by this process of obliteration, they allow to emerge: they screen off anatomy and function, they conceal the organism, in order to raise up before the eyes of those who await the truth the visible relief of forms, with their elements, their mode of distribution and their measurements. (p. 137).

Thus there is no continuity between natural histories and anatomical biology. In fact the two disciplines are separated by a conceptual divide. If Foucault's effort is to be believed, his histories are not imprisoned within the illusions of such hindsight. The past is not a preparation for the present, nor should histories simply lament what the past could not see. Foucault wants to reconstruct what was seen, whatever order was there, on its own terms. Thus he claims for his studies an objectivity, in the sense that they do not merely reflect the present bias. "The history of knowledge can be written only on the basis of what was contemporaneous with it, and certainly not in terms of reciprocal influence, but in terms of conditions and *a prioris* established in time." (p. 208).

Foucault's weapon to dismantle intellectual histories in which truth triumphs over superstition is the historicity and relativity of order and reference. That position is very similar to Laudan's case against the uncritical adoption of "basic ideas" as the units of intellectual history. As Laudan complains, "The concept of space, the idea of the great chain of being, the doctrine of *habeaus corpus*; entities such as these have long been the stock-in-trade, the

primary units of analysis in intellectual history. . . . For all its initial
plausibility, however, there is something profoundly deficient about
focusing on the concept, or (as Lovejoy called it) the 'unit idea'. "[9]
But if, as these critics seem to agree, the traditional methods and
assumptions in the history of ideas fail because the unit of analysis
or basic concept can be questioned as historically relative, how is
epistemological history possible?[10]

Laudan holds that the way in which concepts are historically
embedded can be used to generate an objective account of progress
in human knowledge, and thus a standard of rationality. A standard
is possible even though concepts are not historically autonomous.

> We must not be misled by the fact that most physicists talk
> about space or most political theorists talk about the state,
> into thinking that concepts like "space" and "the state"
> have an historical autonomy about them which allows one
> to explain their historical transformations independently
> of the broader patterns of belief of which the particular
> concepts form only one strand. (p. 184).

Laudan's solution requires a distinction between exegetical and
explanatory history. Exegesis has the traditional descriptive ambi-
tion: "The primary task of the historian of ideas is to get clear about
what people of the past have said and (in sofar as he can get at it)
what they have thought" (p. 178). Laudan is ambiguous on whether
such a purely descriptive history is possible. As I have argued, even
a purely descriptive exegesis will include prescriptive standards as
part of the context in which it functions. Even the most innocuous
historical document, as Popper suggests, requires interpretation.
But even if descriptive history is allowed to pursue its goal, Laudan
prefers explanation.

> There must be, one is inclined to conjecture, something
> about the current methods and presuppositions of the
> history of ideas which accounts for its explanatory bank-
> ruptcy. There are two areas where I am inclined to locate
> difficulties: in the basic units of analysis hitherto utilized
> by the historian of ideas; and in the difficulties that attend
> any effort to explain the beliefs of human agents. (p. 180).

Laudan offers solutions for both limitations. He suggests that historians use the "research tradition" as the unit of analysis, rather than the idea, since the former supplies the "broader framework" or "network of beliefs" in which ideas or concepts inhere. From the view that concepts and problems are embedded in historical research traditions, the question of whether a given concept is unchanging or variable is illusory. Concepts are traditions. An explanation includes more than showing that certain concepts, terms, or ideas reoccur. To be able to judge the claims made or the concepts used, the entire framework must be present. Laudan concludes: "we generally should not appraise or evaluate concepts on a piecemeal basis. Because these larger systems (which I have called 'research traditions') function at any given time as the effective units of acceptance (or rejection), it follows that the intellectual historian – in sofar as he wants to explain the evolving vicissitudes of belief – must take such traditions as his fundamental units for historical analysis" (p. 182).

Laudan's book outlines and defends a problem-solving standard for appraising or judging the rationality of different traditions. For Laudan, the "hallmark" of scientific progress and rationality is success at transforming "anomalous and unsolved empirical problems into solved ones" (p. 18). Though Laudan's criteria of problem-solving allows for the "comparative evaluation" of theories, he still maintains that, apart from this instrumental measure of success, the historical study of rationality encounters shifting standards.

> A mode of argument which one epoch, or "school of thought," views as entirely legitimate and reasonable may be viewed by another era or another intellectual tradition as ill-founded and obscurantist. Neither inductivist nor deductivist theories of rationality leaves the historian any scope for attending to those subtle, temporal shifts in standards of argumentation which continuously confront him in his research. (p. 187)

Both Foucault and Laudan try to overcome the relativism implicit in these "temporal shifts" by expanding the "unit of analysis" from isolated statements to research traditions. Also, both think history of ideas should turn from a naive descriptive enterprise (concerning what was stated) to a presuppositional study (what it was possible to state).

But Laudan avoids relativism concerning the history of knowledge through an instrumental measure of success in problem solving. Laudan, like Foucault, does not try to judge theories on their correspondence to reality or their logical rigor. He appears to accept the historicity of reference and realism. Laudan defines progress only in terms of a tradition's overall success at solving problems. Laudan's solution *is*, therefore, relative because it does depend on the beliefs of the historical agents concerning the nature of problems and solutions.

> In very rough form, we can say that an empirical problem is solved when, within a particular context of inquiry, scientists properly no longer regard it as an unanswered question, i.e. *when they believe they understand* [emphasis added] why the situation propounded by the problem is the way it is. . . ; in determining if a theory solves a problem, *it is irrelevant whether the theory is true or false, well or poorly confirmed*; what counts as a solution to a problem at one time will not necessarily be regarded as such at all times. (pp. 22–23)

Thus an historicist approach leads both Laudan and Foucault to reject scientific realism. Both theories and modes of perception are historical traditions of inquiry. But, unlike Foucault, Laudan concludes that philosophical criticism can adopt a modest instrumental judgment of preferring quantitative success at resolving admittedly historical problem situations. That measure is, however, wholly independent of truth or falsity and to that extent temporal and provisional.

Foucault's argument against realism, on the other hand, rests more on how reference is constituted. Foucault does not consider any pragmatic standards in his theoretical works. While Foucault is suspicious of the function of truth in evaluation theories, he offers no substitute standard for the evaluation or appraisal of systems of knowledge.[11] It is Foucault's frustrating insistence that he can continue to stand on an invisible ground from which to do his critical histories that leads Laudan to dismiss Foucault as a destructive and indefensible relativist.[12]

Foucault does hold, however, that his approach is not viciously relativist. The reason is that Foucault claims to be able to uncover an "historical a priori" in each period he studies. The historical a priori is the common conceptual scheme of representation behind the apparent divergence and controversy in the knowledge of a period. But this deep conceptual scheme is not to be understood as the expression of the Spirit of the Age, consciousness, or human psychology. It is the "structure of the visible" constituting experience. Such structures are not revelations of being or destiny but simply other possible arrangements. Since, for Foucault, there are no necessary or intrinsic links between words and things, this deep conceptualization (which is not conscious for those whose statements it rules) can abruptly change. It is these changes that Foucault refuses to explain completely or view as teleologically directed. Rationality does not progress – even understood as problem solving – because all descriptions and standards are themselves dependent on this historical a priori. Foucault considers epistemological change more a "mutation" than an advance.

Foucault could be understood as holding to a kind of weak Kantianism. He is adopting the position that reference and realism is really constituted at a transcendental level – as Kant called it – in which concept and perception are synthesized. Therefore, objective knowledge can be studied by uncovering historically the different conditions that make knowledge possible. For Foucault, knowledge is fixed in various ways (thus historical), but at any given moment what is empirical is constituted by a system of concepts (thus *a priori*). The term historical a priori fits neither a universal nor relativist view. Foucault claims to be revealing an a priori dimension of knowledge – one which does not determine any teleological growth of knowledge. Knowledge claims are not, therefore, completely relative, since the constitutive or transcendental level makes empirical, arguable and objective knowledge possible.

> This a priori does not consist of a set of constant problems
> . . . providing a ground for . . . progress of rationality; it
> is doubtless not even determined by what is called the
> mentality or the "framework of thought" of any given
> period, if we are to understand by that the historical outline
> of the speculative interests, beliefs or broad theoretical
> options of the time. This *a priori* is what, in a given period,
> delimits in the totality of experience a field of knowledge,

defines the mode of being of the objects that appear in that field, provides man's everyday perception with theoretical powers, and defines the conditions in which he can sustain discourse about things that is recognized to be true. (pp. 157–58).

It is possible to make objective claims about the world, and these claims are not wholly relative even though they are transitory at the constitutive or transcendental level. The system of presupposed concepts can and does change. But the retrospective readings or reconstructions of historians treat these past systems as so much systematic confusion. Foucault sees in these pre-scientific fields different "rigorous and general epistemological arrangements" which encompass the totality of knowledge.

> In any given culture and at any given moment there is always only one *episteme* that defines the conditions of possibility of all knowledge, whether expressed in a theory or silently invested in a practice. . . . And it is these fundamental necessities of knowledge that we must give voice to. (p. 168).

Foucault does not deny that a science of medicine replaced a medical botany or that modern biology replaced natural history. What he challenges is the retrospective judgment that the replacement was progress in rationality through the suppression of muddled superstition. These changes should not be understood as though the present corrects the errors of the past. What changed was the object of knowledge itself. This discontinuity follows from the argument that the empirical order is grounded on a deeper arrangement, an episteme, which while transitory, constitutes objectivity. Thus, "only from a distance," as Foucault often says, can the "mutation" from one episteme to another to be seen.

> [A] body of knowledge is not, in fact, a phenomena of heredity and tradition; and one does not explain how it came about simply by describing the state of knowledge that preceded it and what it has provided by way of – as we say – "original contributions". *The history of knowledge can be written only on the basis of what was contemporaneous with it* [emphasis added], and certainly not in terms of

reciprocal influence, but in terms of conditions and *a prioris* established in time. (p. 208)

The problem with Foucault's analysis is that he also holds that it is impossible to think the common ground of an episteme until it has been replaced by a new arrangement. Foucault condemns inquiry to using the present to judge the past, even though he also condemns that view as a prejudice in traditional history of ideas. Foucault's books have historicist themes because his criticisms and suspicions are possible once a framework no longer holds sway over knowledge. Also, since these changes in the possibility of knowledge are not ruled by any teleological growth or progress, Foucault's own criticisms must reflect some other – but ultimately – arbitrary arrangement. Foucault's whole treatment of philosophy is to read it as reflecting deep epistemological possibilities it can never articulate. For example, Foucault treats modern philosophy as reflecting, after the fact, an epistemological break which makes it possible for both formal systems and history to emerge as objects of knowledge.

> Inversely, a new philosophical space was to emerge in the place where the objects of Classical knowledge dissolved. . . . Thus the two great forms of modern philosophic reflection were established. The first questions the relations between logic and ontology; it proceeds by the paths of formalization and encounters, in a new form, the problem of *mathesis*. The second questions the relations of signification and time; . . . it brings back into prominence the themes and methods of *interpretations*. (p. 207)

What Foucault calls the great philosophical theme of "relations of signification and time" is clearly what I have been calling historicism. Historicism explains different modes of representation as the products of history, society, or the evolution of culture. Foucault is arguing that historicism, relativism, and scepticism are possible *in their modern forms* because of a previous epistemological change whose repercussions are just now becoming visible. Foucault thus situates in history this relativist perspective on knowledge. In this way, Foucault intends to deflate the importance of philosophy. Historicism is not a philosophical position to be argued for or criticized. It is a reflection of the limits of the modern episteme. Historicism concludes that all knowledge claims are subjective because it suddenly is able to think the possibility of diverse histories and cultures. Philosophy then seeks to understand and comprehend this underlying diversity.

> All knowledge is rooted in a life, a society, and a language that have a history; and it is in that very history that knowledge finds the element enabling it to communicate with other forms of life, other types of society, other significations; that is why historicism always implies a certain philosophy, or at least a methodology, of living comprehension (in the element of the *Lebenswelt*), of interhuman communication (against a background of social structures), and hermeneutics (as the re-apprehension through the manifest meaning of the discourse of another meaning at once secondary and primary, that is, more hidden but also more fundamental). (pp. 372–73)

Foucault, like Laudan, condemns historicism for this solely exegetical task of describing what Foucault calls "positivities." Foucault argues that the historicist project is impossible. Historicism claims to represent the diversity of thought while treating all past representations as the expression of a limited culture or society. For Foucault, historicism helplessly reflects a circularity inherent in the modern episteme of knowledge by perspective and time.

Thus Foucault's book ends with this confusing yet prophetic dilemma. The book Foucault has written is possible because a new "space," as he likes to say, has emerged. But that historicist defense allows Foucault to forego any argument. In fact, he fills his works with almost obsessively detailed expository descriptions of past systems of knowledge. Foucault implies, therefore, that all philosophical and critical arguments are illusory. Announcing the dawn of a new order as the condition for possibility of the very books he has written is meant to disarm his critics in advance. Arguments are unnecessary, since the only clarification possible must await the perspective of distant, future eyes on this new episteme.

But, on his own terms, Foucault's reconstructive histories are not descriptions. His expositions are written from "somewhere."

The vantage point is, as Foucault argues, not accessible to the author or reader. Any period will find the presuppositions behind its mode of representation invisible. It is only the historical "distance" Foucault often appeals to that allows him to dismantle past texts. Such an "owl of Minerva" advantage, and granted there is never a final truth of the past, is simply in tension with Foucault's repeated claim that the past must not be read anachronistically or retrospectively. Foucault's criticisms of traditional history of ideas now seem unconvincing and unclear in view of his own final capitulation to the present perspective. On what basis, if both truth and pragmatic concerns are explicitly excluded by Foucault, can he dismiss the various histories of ideas he criticizes? If all thought is a prisoner of its contemporaneous episteme or all commentary merely description, how can there be criticism? Once Foucault excludes the possibility of reflection or philosophical argument then the only reason for his work's arrangement or analysis must be a "whiggish" adherence to the perspective of the present. But is that not the assumption or bias Foucault began by rejecting? Foucault's grand announcements about *The Order of Things* seem nothing more than a belated historicism.

Foucault cannot exempt himself from the "positive unconscious" that he claims always rules knowledge. Without it, *The Order of Things* is not and could not be a description of various epistemes in Western culture. Foucault is speaking from some arrangement or perspective that makes this knowledge possible. If his work does not rest on the truth, the natural order of things, or some psychological insight, how are Foucault's selections and criticisms different? In a later writing, Foucault realizes the dilemma in his claim to escape the illusions and limits of our tradition: "It is not possible for us to describe our own archive, since it is within these rules that we speak, since it is that which gives to what we can say – and to itself, the object of our discourse – its modes of appearance, its forms of existence and coexistence, its system of accumulation, historicity, and disappearance."[14] The project of clarifying epistemological foundations is once again submerged in history.

In Foucault's explicitly philosophical work *The Archaeology of Knowledge* he did attempt an interesting, though largely ignored, answer to the problems raised by his earlier works. I will consider that work in the next chapter, but, for the present, I have treated

Foucault as arguing for what might be called transcendental historicism. By transcendental I mean that all knowledge is possible on the basis of a presupposed synthesis of conception and perception, and by historical I mean that these perspectives are understood as traditions. Concepts are "micro-institutions," as Stephen Toulmin has put it. Foucault's investigations are meant to reconstruct these perspectives, hence the need for rigorously criticizing the assumptions of the present about teleology, realism, or reference. But Foucault also, inconsistently I believe, treats his own reconstructions as beyond perspectivism and relativism because they are written at the "right" historical moment, the moment in which a past episteme is crumbling and a new arrangement has yet to solidify. This argument offers an Hegelian notion of progress in knowledge in which systems of thought become progressively more self-conscious by reflecting upon and building upon the systems of the past. Of course, given Foucault's disdain for argument it is difficult to prove that his work rests on a revival of the notions of accumulation and progress that he tried to discredit. To go beyond historicism, Foucault must confront the traditional philosophical debates concerning scepticism and relativism without dismissing them as so many cultural expressions.

6

Objective Mind

Does classification represent the world or simply a system of categories? Do historical changes in classifications represent corrections leading to true knowledge of the world or simply diverse, equally valid orders? Are there universal classificatory guidelines or are categories the product of relative criteria such as utility or familiarity? The relativist implications of these kind of questions were already confronted by Plato who formulated a similar issue with the "butcher metaphor" in *The Statesman* and *The Phaedrus*. In both dialogues, Socrates argues against the sophistic position that division or classification is arbitrary. He compares the activity of classification in knowledge to butchering an animal. To carve the animal at its joints, along what the dialogues call the "natural divisions," is like classifying correctly. Socrates asks us to contrast this technique with the unskilled person who simply hacks away at the meat on the bone. The failure to carve is the failure to follow the divisions or separations that really belong to the object. Socrates even holds that there is an economy in the single correct division: "To bisect . . . according to natural division . . . we must in every case divide into the minimum number of divisions the structure permits."[1] In *The Phaedrus* he says: "We divide into forms, following the objective articulations; we are not to attempt to hack off parts like a clumsy butcher."[2] The lesson is that we cannot divide up, classify, or cut up the world just any way we please. There *is* an objective articulation and, thus, we must aim to mirror that articulation in our concepts. With these arguments Plato attacked the sophistic position that the concepts of physics, cosmology, and astronomy were inherently conventional and human choices, for which there was no ultimate justification. Plato's appeal to simplicity or economy was not, as it might appear today, a pragmatic argument against conceptual diversity since Plato held that simplicity was a sign of truth. Later in the history of science simplicity became a substitute for the truth.[3] Plato's distinction between matters of opinion (*doxa*) and matters of knowledge (*episteme*) demanded that conflicting claims about the world must be reconciled by a knowledge that reflects reality's structure rather than arbitrary opinion.

Plato's answer to sophistic conventionalism is virtually impossible to revive today because of doubts that the world even has "natural divisions," let alone ones revealed by purely theoretical inquiry. In modern philosophy theories are often presented as historical perspectives or "versions" of the world, even where they are simple, useful, and "rational." Modern philosophy begins, as Foucault suggests, by accepting that reality may accommodate diverse accounts and therefore often seeks some *subjective* foundation, such as belief, utility or instrumental success.

Both Foucault and Popper have, however, proposed a study of theories without subjective foundations. Foucault calls it freeing discourse from the "anthropological theme" and Popper considers this objective account of knowledge as based on the distinction between the content of knowledge and any particular beliefs, perceptions, or psychological states. The products of language, such as theories, hypotheses, and statements, are autonomous. By severing the relationship between theory and belief both Foucault and Popper claim to solve the problems of relativism and historicism.

Consider, for example, Foucault's anti-Platonist attitude toward classification. In contrast with Plato's "butcher metaphor," Foucault denies that classificatory systems are either natural or intrinsic. He suggests that classification and thus objects of knowledge are produced by normative, anonymous "practices." These practices, which do not correspond to the world, undergo abrupt historical shifts. Foucault does not conclude, however, that classification is wholly arbitrary and subjective. Though it is not regulated by correspondence with the world there are "rules" (albeit historical ones) for classificatory and conceptual schemes. These rules, which Foucault discovers through reconstruction, are not reducible to consciousness, subjectivity, or human psychology. In fact,

Foucault suggests that acts of perception and belief are made possible by objective knowledge, in what Foucault calls discursive formations.

All assumptions about the relationship between theories, intentions, and physical objects have to be reexamined, and, with them, notions of "subject" and "rationality." No longer ask, Foucault recommends, "What was the meaning or intention behind what was written or said?" but "Why these particular groupings of statements at that time and not others?"

Foucault begins his reexamination by distinguishing between sentences, propositions, and what he calls statements.[4] Though each term concerns functions of language and communication, the new history of ideas Foucault calls "archaeology" must keep these functions distinct. Archaeology studies the production of "statements," a domain prior to the distinction between objectivity and subjectivity.

Foucault separates statements from logical propositions. A logical proposition is neither a necessary nor sufficient condition for their being a statement. For example the phrases "No one heard" and "It is true that no one heard" are identical formulations from the logical point of view. But Foucault argues that at the level of statements "these two formations are not equivalent or interchangeable. They cannot occupy the same place on the plane of discourse, nor can they belong to exactly the same group of statements" (p. 81).

He suggests that "No one heard" as the first line of a novel and "It is true that no one heard" as part of a dialogue function as different statements (because they are part of distinct discursive formations). Thus, propositional structure is distinct from what Foucault calls a statement's "enunciative function."

Foucault then suggests that if propositional structure is too restrictive the historian might simply take the sentence or grammatical unit as basic. What the historian of ideas studies is then the sentences of historical authors. But Foucault wants to include among cases of knowledge and discourse such things as classificatory tables, geneaological trees, account books, balance of trade calculations. All these are statement, in Foucault's use of the term, but are either not expressed in sentences or are incapable of being expressed in a finite group of sentences.

> Lastly, a graph, a growth curve, an age pyramid, a distribution cloud are all statements: any sentences that may accompany them are merely interpretation or commentary; they are in no way an equivalent: this is proved by the fact that, in a great many cases, only an infinite number of sentences could equal all the elements that are explicitly formulated in this sort of statement. It would not appear to be possible, therefore, to define a statement by the grammatical characteristics of the sentence. (p. 82)

Foucault finally asks whether a statement is what the philosopher of language J.L. Austin called a "speech act." Foucault points out, however, that the term "speech act" is used in modern philosophy in many different ways. Sometimes it refers to the speaker's intention or beliefs. But statements are not reducible to intended meanings. Though a statement and a speech act are both events in the world, such actions as promising, ordering, decreeing, contracting, observing, or agreeing can be studied as part of discursive formations wholly apart from how subjects use these formulations or what they intend by them.[5]

Foucault thus holds that a speech act is simply a grammatical form and is distinct from a statement. Linguistic actions such as promising may involve different statements or occur within different discursive formations. What the intellectual historian studies is the discourse itself rather than linguistic usage.

> When one wishes to individualize statements, one cannot therefore accept unreservedly any of the models borrowed from grammar, logic, or "analysis." In all three cases, one realizes that the criteria proposed are too numerous and too heavy, that they limit the extent of the statement, and that although the statement sometimes takes on the forms described and adjusts itself to them exactly, it does not always do so: one finds statements lacking in legitimate propositional structure; one finds statements where one cannot recognize a sentence; one finds more statements than one can isolate speech acts. (p. 84)

The statement is what is left over, the "residual materiality" of signs, when the propositional, grammatical, and functional aspects are removed. Statements are as distinct and autonomous as "things." While Foucault grants that statements only exist where there is language, he maintains: "Language (*langue*) and statement are not at the same level of existence; and one cannot say that there are statements in the same way as one says that there are languages" (p. 85).

Why does he so carefully distinguish statements from sentences and propositions? One reason is that otherwise the history of knowledge would be unintelligible. If the units of knowledge were ultimately propositional or grammatical, disputes would either be trivial, that is, cases of ungrammatical sentences or logical errors, or impossible. Historical change in knowledge would be intentional, a matter of will and decision. Also, errors would be corrected by simple and mechanical rules. But changes at the discursive level are not over correct formulation of sentences or propositions. For Foucault, these changes are neither automatic nor conscious. In Foucault's archaeology of knowledge the study of epistemes require neither the study of thinking subjects nor the referent or object.

> But nor is the *correlate* of the statement a state of things or a relation capable of verifying the proposition. . . . the *correlate* of the statement is a group of domains in which such objects may appear and to which such relations may be assigned: it would, for example, be a domain of material objects . . . fictitious objects . . . spatial and geographical localizations . . . and secret kinships. (p. 91)

Foucault wants to broaden the documentation of knowledge. He includes the random numbers used by a statistician or the series of letters appearing in a typewriting manual as statements. Foucault is trying to isolate a level of analysis that somehow resides neither in the physical events of the natural world nor in the intentions or beliefs of human subjects. For every epoch the historian can reconstruct an anonymous, replicating, and objective knowledge. The discursive system which makes knowledge possible can be studied independently of linguistic forms or human psychology. Statement are autonomous from language and, like "real" objects, from human experience.

> The statement exists therefore neither in the same way as
> a language (*langue*) (although it is made up of signs that are
> definable in their individuality only within a natural or arti-
> ficial linguistic system), nor in the same way as the objects
> presented to perception (although it is always endowed
> with a certain materiality, and can always be situated in
> accordance with spatio-temporal coordinates). (p. 86)

Discursive formations turn out to be not so much units of analysis
as practices, operations, or systems constituting the concepts,
objects, and subjects that are normally taken as the units of
knowledge. For Foucault, the constitutive level is autonomous
and thus this possibility for knowledge claims can be treated as
anonymous, as prior to the formation of subjectivity.[6]

Foucault may have been led to these views about the production
of knowledge, apart from subjectivity, by certain arguments from
Heidegger. Heidegger treats scientific research as inquiry into
an already "projected plan for nature." Science investigates a
"circumscribed object-sphere" and the historical constitution of a
sphere of objects available for representation is *prior* to the acts of
observation, explanation, and accumulation of evidence. Heidegger
thus restricts the role of experimentation. "But physical science
does not first become research through experiment; rather, on the
contrary, experiment first becomes possible where and only where
the knowledge of nature has been transformed into research."[7]

The representation of the world, therefore, is "anticipated" by
a "ground-plan" which constitutes the appropriate object-sphere.
Heidegger seems to hold that these object-spheres change in history
and that modern observation, for instance, "remains essentially
different even when ancient and medieval observation also works
with number and measurement." The deep study of knowledge is
not in terms of the object-sphere but the underlying constitution or
projection of objectivity.

Though Foucault treats these object-spheres as arbitrary he also
views them as rule-like social practices. Foucault does not like
Heidegger overcome the historical diversity of object-spheres by
investigating the being of objects. The historical traditions of
representation alone interest Foucault.

Foucault's concern is with a more restricted and historical question: How are groups of statements unified into a discipline?[8] Why are certain statements grouped together as biology and others as economics? Foucault considers four answers to this question. The first answer is that statements are unified when they all refer to the same object. Foucault replies to this answer with his anti-realist views about theoretical terms. The "object" that a system of knowledge posits is not some piece of reality – a point Foucault claims to have already demonstrated in his history of mental illness.

> But I soon realized that the unity of the object "madness" does not enable one to individualize a group of statements. . . . It would certainly be a mistake to try to discover what could have been said of madness at a particular time by interrogating the being of madness itself . . . ; the object presented as their correlative by medical statements of the seventeenth or eighteenth century is not identical with the object that emerges in legal sentences or police action . . . ; we are not dealing with the same madmen. (p. 32)

Foucault suggests that all theoretical terms are like madness (it is not just a bad example). The object of theory is constituted; hence, realism is not the explanation but the result of a disciplinary unification.

He then considers a second answer, that statements are unified into a discipline by *style*, which emphasizes a distinction between descriptive and metaphoric prose. As I noted earlier in terms of Foucault's studies of medicine, for him, a discipline emerges when a distinctive descriptive style dominates inquiry.

> It seemed to me, for example, that from the nineteenth century medical science was characterized not so much by its objects or concepts as by a certain *style*, a certain constant manner of statement. For the first time, medicine no longer consisted of a group of traditions, observations, and heterogeneous practices, but of a corpus of knowledge that presupposed *the same way of looking at things*

[emphasis added], the same division of the perceptual field, the same analyses of the pathological fact . . . ; in short, it seemed to me that medicine was organized as a series of descriptive statements. (p. 33)

But Foucault's study of medicine was meant to show that no field is purely exegetical and thus cannot be differentiated by this stylistic element. Traditionally, historians of ideas assume that a certain "way of seeing" means reliable knowledge. But for Foucault description is a form of pedagogy. It is only an illusion of hindsight that makes description seem neutral. Since, in Foucault's account, description is epistemically relative, a style is determined or shaped by a discursive system and does not itself differentiate knowledge from opinion. A discursive formation makes it possible to distinguish between the metaphorical and the descriptive, but there is no pure style behind that distinction.

The third possible answer unifies fields of knowledge around concepts such as matter, life, the economy, the state which define the same subject matter. Foucault's reply should now be obvious. The search for the "conceptual architecture" of a field fails because concepts are historical and, therefore, are not continuous. On the contrary, traditional history of ideas, as Foucault criticizes it, perpetuates the illusion of continuity in intellectual life through concepts like "matter" in physics or the "state" in economics. But it is not the concept which creates the discipline, and investigation of concepts will not produce knowledge. There are no essential concepts, only historical frameworks.

Finally, Foucault considers whether knowledge is simply unified around themes.

> Could one not, for example, constitute as a unity everything that has constituted the evolutionist theme from Buffon to Darwin? A theme that in the first instance was more philosophical, closer to cosmology than to biology; a theme that directed research from afar rather than named, regrouped, and explained results; a theme that always presupposed more than one was aware of, but which, on the basis of this fundamental choice, forcibly transformed into discursive knowledge what had been outlined as a hypothesis or as a necessity. (p. 35)

Foucault rejects the analysis because a single theme, such as evolution, can be encompassed by different discursive statements. The theme of evolution in the group of statements that makes a Diderot possible is not the same as that of Darwin. The theme provides no continuity. Whereas in the eighteenth century, Foucault argues, evolution meant a continuous table of species "forming a continuum laid down at the outset," by the nineteenth century evolution meant "the analysis of the modes of interaction between an organism whose elements are interdependent and an environment that provides its real conditions of life. A single theme [evolution], but based on two types of discourse" (p. 36).

If the study of knowledge cannot be done through objects, concepts, styles, themes, or subjects how does one proceed? Foucault is trying to make a case for the autonomy of discourse. He wants to demonstrate that discourse cannot be reduced to a more primitive level. As he says in a later writing: "A type of rationality, a way of thinking, a program, a technique, a totality of rational and coordinated efforts, of defined and pursued objectives, of instruments for achieving those objectives, etc., *all these are real* [emphasis added] even if they do not pretend to be reality itself nor society as a whole."[9]

Foucault's point is that often the term "real" is given a restrictive sense that the historian of ideas accepts uncritically. Philosophical arguments about what is or is not "the furniture of the world" are always made within theoretical or metaphysical assumptions. Embedded in their own historical contexts, these arguments prejudice intellectual history. If it is assumed that a theoretical discourse is not real then the inquiry will search for its real causes. Foucault wants historians to reject this traditional ontology distinguishing between mental states and material processes, demanding in advance that all abstract entities need material referents.

The view that rationality is not just a psychological state or reducible to either subjectivity or a formal model is certainly an important and defensible position in modern philosophy. Foucault's *Archaeology of Knowledge* turns this point into an ambitious program for reforming the humanities.

Foucault understands the study of knowledge as reconstructive. Knowledge is a certain kind of historical activity or practice. The central question for Foucault is not the distinction between science and ideology but the framework that sustains and situates that distinction in a given historical context. Thus his aim is not merely to describe the history of knowledge but to analyse how knowledge is produced "What the analysis of the episteme questions is not its right to be a science, but the fact that it exists. . . . the point at which it separates itself off from all the philosophies of knowledge (*connaissance*) is that it relates this fact not to the authority of an original act of giving, which establishes in a transcendental subject the fact and the right, but to the processes of a historical practice" (p. 192).

Foucault dismisses any philosophical justification of knowledge and methodology. By arguing that knowledge cannot be reduced to belief, subjectivity, origin, or materiality, he intends to demonstrate that there are no pure criteria of rationality. Rationality as justified belief is always relative.

But subjectivity is used in different ways by Foucault. In one essay he shows that the idea of the "author" is arbitrary and conventional.[10] In other places he expresses the wish that he could write histories of knowledge without using proper names and mentions, wistfully, how much more he learns from the minor anonymous tracts in the history of knowledge than from Hume or Kant. All of these comments suggest that Foucault means by subjectivity the relationship of knowledge to specific *historical figures*. When he attacks Kant's notion of a transcendental subjectivity he holds that such an intellectual strategy reflects cultural conventions concerning "authorship" and the "authentic origins" of knowledge. Like Popper, he thinks that traditional philosophy continually asks the wrong question: Where does knowledge come from?

But given these reasonable arguments for the objectivity of knowledge, has Foucault established a separation of discourse from subjective experience? The problem is one of Foucault's access to this objective knowledge. The documents of the history of knowledge are the material inscriptions, authored or unauthored, collected by design or accident, and generated by individuals, cultures, or institutions. Whether the selection is anonymous or not is relatively unimportant. The issue is whether these sets of statements – which Foucault claims are regulated and restricted by culture – can be studied divorced from human interests. Without subjectivity there may continue to be statements already recorded in books and libraries, but there can be no problem situation for reconstruction. The study of knowledge would have to be purely descriptive. In dismissing the role of interests and practical reason behind the constitution of objectivity, Foucault thinks he has resolved the threat of relativism and historicism – but he has done so at the cost of making his very project unintelligible. Without subjectivity knowledge ceases to have the pedagogical, institutional, or practical functions Foucault emphasizes. The result is the very fallacy of traditional history of ideas Foucault began by rejecting.

Foucault can only demand once more that intellectual history abandon guidelines such as empirical adequacy or simplicity as the vantage point for reconstructions. Foucault is left steering between all the alternatives.

> In other words, the archaeological description of discourses is deployed in the dimension of a general history; it . . . tries to show how the autonomy of discourse and its specificity nevertheless do not give it the status of pure ideality and total historical independence; what it wishes to uncover is the particular level in which history can give place to definite types of discourse, which have their own type of historicity, and which are related to a whole set of various historicities. (pp. 164–65)

Foucault's argument seems to rest on a rather traditional distinction between abstract discourses and their material institutions. Statements are autonomous, but neither pure nor ideal. Foucault wants objectivity to be studied at the level of the constitution of object-spheres. But since Foucault argues at length that such knowledge is not a matter of essences, intrinsic distinctions, reference, or psychological awareness, he must give some characterization of this level if his arguments are meant to avoid both subjectivism and scepticism.

Foucault claims that there are rules for the production of knowledge, but that these rules are neither logical nor psychological. That appears to leave rules for the production of knowledge by cultural convention. Thus a defense of the objectivity of knowledge against claims that it reduces to a subject's awareness or mental state does not also block the argument that knowledge is a vast cultural ideology. That is precisely why Hilary Putnam, for instance, can see no other result in Foucault's analyses but this historical and cultural relativism.

Foucault's defense of objective knowledge seems, to use Imre Lakatos's phrase, to lack "hard teeth." It responds to psychologism and empiricism, but not historicism. A defense of objective knowledge parallel to Foucault's anti-subjectivism was proposed by Popper. The history of science, he argues, should investigate theories not as thought by individuals but simply theories as such, as objects in and of themselves, in what Popper calls "objective problem situations."[11] Theories, argues Popper, belong to a domain that falls neither within that of material objects nor that of states of belief or mental acts.[12] Theories are part of a third domain in which Popper includes the contents of journals, texts in libraries, computer tapes, and even logarithm tables; this domain – which does not require a physical manifestation – also includes arguments, narratives and conjectures, not as thought but existing autonomously as objects. Though third world objects (such as books and paintings) are manifested as physical things, their third-world status rests on a content which is replicated with the physical object but independent of and not identical to its material existence.

Popper distinguishes the first world of physical objects from mental states, beliefs, consciousness, and intentions that he calls the second world. Behavior is, of course, also a physical state of the body, but as motive, intention, or project it is not physiological. Popper had supported a version of the mind-body dualism in his arguments against scientific determinism. He extends that position into a three-level analysis of objects, minds, and abstractions. Each level of reality is autonomous. Popper grants that third world objects are the "products" of human activity, but he rejects certain conclusions drawn from this admission.

First, it should not be assumed that if something is not a physical object it must be a mental state. The third world object, though it is the product of human activity, has the kind of objectivity and independence from mental states of a physical object. But these objects are neither wholly physical and natural nor wholly immaterial, in the manner of emotions, feelings or intentions. The number system, Popper's favorite example of a third-world object, has independence from psychological states but nevertheless is not a physical object. Though often given physical expression in writing, the uses and functions of the number system are separable from any arbitrary embodiment, as well as any beliefs it engenders among subjects who use the number system. Though not physical, the number system produces effects in the world and Popper considers these effects proof of third-world reality. These effects are not mediated through conscious awareness.

Second, it should not be assumed that what is not material is not objective. Third world objects generate unintended consequences, even though they are not physical objects. We tend to assume, incorrectly Popper argues, that palpable results are always the effect of physical objects. But decisions and reasons, along with symbolic systems, can cause things to happen, including events not intended by those decisions or reasons. Popper's position is anti-reductionist on two fronts, against reducing psychological states to physical states and then reducing abstract knowledge to psychological states. The number system is not a belief and not a thing, it is objective knowledge.

> Let us look at the theory of numbers. I believe (. . .) that even natural numbers are the work of men, the product of human language and of human thought. Yet there is an infinity of such numbers, more than will ever be pronounced by men or used by computers. . . .
>
> But what is even more interesting, unexpected problems arise as an unintended byproduct of the sequence of natural numbers; . . . These problems are clearly *autonomous*. They are in no sense made by us; rather they are *discovered* by us; and in this sense they exist, undiscovered, before their discovery. . . .
>
> This explains why the third world which, in its origin, is our product, is *autonomous* in what may be called its ontological status.[13]

Popper does not restrict the objectivity or autonomy of knowledge to true knowledge or that in correspondence with worlds one or two. The third world includes false theories, imaginative narratives, possible conjectures, and non-representational forms such as music and poetry.

In trying to understand Popper's argument for such an expanded ontology I will follow his own suggestion of reconstructing the problem situation he faced with this conjecture. I am suggesting that, in part, this new ontology was a response to the threats of relativism and scepticism which Popper saw emerging from his study of historical reconstruction and interpretation theory. By placing knowledge in the third world, Popper hoped in effect to revive a version of Plato's attack on *doxa*. Though Popper could not agree with Platonism's eternal ideal forms and claim to certainty, he could agree with Plato that knowledge is "real" and present independently of belief, assent, assertion, and agreement. "Knowledge in the objective sense is *knowledge without a knower*: it is *knowledge without a knowing subject*."[14]

"Knowledge without a subject" might appear to clash with Popper's position that: "The first and third world cannot interact save through the intervention of the second world, the world of subjective and personal experiences," and that, "it is possible to accept the reality or (as it may be called) the autonomy of the third world, as at the same time to admit that the third world originates as a product of human activity."[15] This tension, however, is only apparent.[16] The point is that the beliefs or opinions of an historical figure do not change the content of a theory and that means that theory, as a third-world object, transcends historical context. The cultural context of a theory or the conditions that led to belief or disbelief in it add nothing to its content. Further, theoretical criticism can occur with or without the cultural context. Of course, reflection on theoretical knowledge must be *mediated* by subjects who have beliefs and who exist in concrete historical situations, but that in no way, Popper holds, qualifies or relativizes the objectivity and independent reality of theoretical knowledge.

As I have indicated, the third world contains non-representational and non-scientific examples. Mozart's piano sonatas are not identical to their spatio-temporal performance, nor are they reducible to those objects in the world (books and manuscripts) and mental states associated with them. Though they were produced by an individual in a cultural context, their third-world reality is what alone makes the music replicable and autonomous from those particular conditions.

The sonatas are abstractly present whether performed or not and are automatically reproduced, irrespective of historical beliefs, in every physical copy of the sonatas. Further, the sonatas have discoverable properties which were not intended or thought by their author, nor necessarily understood by any culture, but are nonetheless *there* and automatically reproduced with the physical copies. The sonatas are, among other things, content waiting to be discovered: knowledge. Third world autonomy is fortunate, Popper argues, otherwise knowledge would be as transient and historically relative as a subject's beliefs and opinions.

Popper uses the idea of "autonomy" in a manner similar to that of Nelson Goodman in his distinction between "allographic" and "autographic" works of art.[17] Goodman, in a discussion of forgeries and fakes, notes that certain works cannot have forgeries. These "allographic" works have no original, but are, in effect, all copies. Works of music exist in all performances and all manuscript copies. A performance of Mozart is not a fake if the manuscript is not original, nor is it a forgery if the performance is very poor. The performance can perhaps, due to wrong notes and skipped passages, cease at some point to be "Mozart." Paintings, on the contrary, are "autographic" because they are unique, unrepeatable objects. All copies of a painting are forgeries because there is only one authentic original.

Novels, for instance, are allographic. There is a first printing or an author's manuscript, but even assuming that such an original exists all further copies are neither forgeries nor inauthentic. Once again, if there are enough misprints or typos the novel simply ceases to be a copy rather than a fake or forgery. In effect, some cultural objects are inherently reproducible.[18] The connection to epistemology is that knowledge as objective is this disposition toward replication and thus independent of any particular "carrier" of knowledge.

Goodman accounts for this difference in objects by holding that allographic works have a "notation system," and, thus, copies are all real cases of the work as long as there is "sameness of spelling" within the notation system. But autographic works do not have a notation system and even the best, most accurate copy of the *La Gioconda* is not the *La Gioconda*, whereas the sloppiest manuscript copy of a Mozart piano sonata, as long as it maintains the same notational designations, *is* the Mozart piano sonata. Popper includes all these objects in his third-world realm but, as Goodman's distinction shows, the aspect of replicability that Popper uses as an argument for the autonomy of the third world only applies to certain objectivities. Popper invests this entire realm of "exosomatic systems of control"[19] with a separate reality. But Goodman shows that, without falling into psychologism, he can account for such "replication" without special ontological commitments.

Popper duplicates all cultural objects because, unlike Goodman, he feels compelled to explain the fact of replication by positing for such cultural objects two realities. But is the third-world reality accessible apart from the physical existence of the object and my mental awareness of it? I am aware that Popper opposes the notion of verification, but I am not demanding that his ontological statements be verifiable. However, positing ontological entities is a strategy and should be compared to alternative accounts. Do Popper's points about knowledge, objectivity, and culture demand this third world conjecture?

Goodman's approach does not require that cultural objects be reduced to psychological expressions, yet he still accounts for replication and autonomy. Of course, Goodman's view does not turn his interest in aesthetic objects or science into an argument against relativism.[20] Goodman's question "When is art?," for example, grows out of a recognition that the replicability of cultural objects and their relativity to context are compatible positions. Thus while anti-psychologism does not require a third-world ontology, it may be true that Popper's effort to extend this argument into a reply to scepticism and relativism does require that added ontological complication.

Popper, like Foucault, believes that interpretation theory has fallen prey to subjectivism because of the misleading analogy that every text requires a reader. This analogy leads to the conclusion that a book no one reads reduces to "just paper with black marks." Popper concludes that hermeneutics and interpretation theories adopt a pseudo-problem, namely the effort to identify and preserve the correct reading. For Popper, this incorrect problem leads theories of interpretation into efforts of eliminating errors. But all texts, for Popper, are misinterpreted, there is no absolutely correct reading and precisely because of the continual fate of misreading and misunderstanding knowledge remains possible and objective.

> Moreover, a book, even a library, need not even have been written by anybody: a series of books of logarithms, for example, may be produced or printed by a computer. . . . Yet each of these figures contains what I call "objective knowledge"; . . . I should say that almost every book is like this: it contains objective knowledge, true or false, useful or useless; and *whether anybody ever reads it and really grasps its contents is almost accidental* [emphasis added] . . . there would always be plenty of misunderstandings and misinterpretations; and it is not the actual and somewhat accidental avoidance of misunderstanding which turns black spots on white paper into a book, or an instance of knowledge in the objective sense. Rather it is something more abstract. It is its possibility or potentiality of being understood, its dispositional character of being under-stood or interpreted, or misunderstood or misinterpreted, which makes a thing a book. And this potentiality or dispo-sition exists whether or not it is actualized or realized.[21]

This argument is an extremely important contribution to the study of historical interpretation. Popper is holding that the objective content of knowledge persists without any physical manifestation or subjective awareness as a "disposition." Popper is not defending the somewhat mundane point that books as physical objects are autonomous. He is arguing that their abstract content is autonomous.

Imagine a book surviving the destruction of all artifacts and human accomplishments. Popper is arguing that its knowledge, not just its material existence, is an objective, real content that persists whether the book will ever be read or understood.

But this example shows a difficulty in Popper's insight. If by saying that books survive we mean the content rather than just the physical object, then what must survive in addition to the object is a "network" or cultural practice that provides access to the work's content. It is this practice that embodies what Popper calls a "disposition" to understand the book's "inside." But if the book is supposed to survive with no context or framework Popper cannot still assume it is a "book," in that special non-physical sense of having a "dispositional character."

His example begs the question. After all, Popper's suggestion is that the disposition exists independently of any reading and that the reader, from any interest or perspective discovers content in the book. One does not have to disagree with that reasonable point to argue, just as persuasively, that by the phrase "discovers content" all that is meant is that the reader learns to understand the book's meaning by mastering some tradition, context, or practice of interpretation. The notion of "learning to master a tradition" does not require positing another reality over and above natural objects and human subjectivity.

Popper's refutation of relativism, however, requires more than his argument against psychologism. He posits in the third world an objective logic of problem solving. The third world is a domain, not of what persons believe about theories, but of objective consequences and implications. Thus third-world analysis escapes historical questions about meaning and belief because theoretical content, apart from the subjective intent, is a discoverable reality. Problem solving transcends historical diversity.[22]

But Popper has introduced two slightly different pictures. In one, third-world objectivity is a real object which is literally "discovered," the way in which a new continent is discovered. In the second, third-world objectivity is a study of logical implication or possibility. Though the first does require an expanded ontology, the second picture does not necessitate such a conclusion. If Popper is to identify the aim of science with this third world search for truth, he cannot collapse logical possibilities and empirical discovery. Such a view would reintroduce a Platonic conception of mirroring ideal objectivities and thus collapse physical and formal inquiry. Popper opposes the reduction of knowledge to mental or physiological states by positing a realm of theory in which scientific, aesthetic, and formal objects are all one.

To answer the claim of historicism, Popper shows how the objective emergence of knowledge is guided toward an end, namely truth, which is continuous across frameworks or conceptual schemes. But Popper cannot show such growth either directly by correspondence or by some metaphysical teleology in nature or history. Such positions would repeat the "poverty" of historicism and essentialism. Popper calls his own view an emergent or evolutionary theory of knowledge, where error elimination by the "natural selection" of conjectures produces growth and progress in knowledge which is neither historically nor psychologically relative.

As an example of how evolutionary epistemology can produce non-relativistic reconstructions, Popper discusses the case of Galileo's theory of tides. For Popper, the objective problem situation for Galileo's theory was the need for a mechanistic defense of Copernicanism. Galileo attempted to provide such an argument by explaining the tides through accelerations due to the earth's motion. In understanding this objective problem situation Popper dismisses any speculation about Galileo's emotions, beliefs, or motives. Popper reconstructs the inquiry on the basis of a third-world object, namely the program of explaining the Copernican system mechanically rather than in geometric terms. Galileo had, according to Popper's reconstruction, succeeded with this program in his account of accelerated motion during free-fall and the law of inertia. Thus Galileo was rational, in the third-world sense, to proceed with this model for explaining tides. By saying he was rational Popper does not mean that Galileo actually believed in or conceived of such a program and its implications. Nor does Popper have to show any evidence that such a program was held by Galileo or any other historical figure of that time. It may even be argued that it was historically impossible for Galileo to view his own research as a fallible "conjecture." Popper might agree with that historical judgment, but maintain that it remains a logical possibility of reconstruction given our present perspective.

First, Popper indicates that the purpose of a reconstruction is to *understand* the objective problem situation, rather than what Galileo thought was at issue. Galileo's problem situation, as reconstructed historically, includes a background theoretical framework which either Galileo was not aware of or viewed as unproblematic (for example, certain assumptions may have appeared "natural"). Of course, our whole retrospective reconstruction depends on what Galileo could not know. In fact reconstruction must always be from a vantage point other than that of the historical participant. But since there never is an end to knowledge, reconstructions go on continually.

Galileo was committed to the circular motion of planets and suspicious of Kepler's arguments for elliptical orbits and the influence of the moon on the tides. But his commitment to this ultimately mistaken view of the tides, and opposition to Kepler's occult explanation of tides, is not explained in Popper's reconstruction by some psychological fascination with circularity, nor as a cultural ideology. Rather, Galileo's suspicions of Kepler can be reconstructed as the rational implications of a purely mechanical defense of Copernicanism. Popper's hypothesis makes Galileo's rejection of Kepler comprehensible and rational to us.

> Thus we are led by the analysis of Galileo's problem situation to justify the rationality of Galileo's method on several points in which he has been criticized by various historians: and thus we are led to a better *historical understanding* of Galileo. Psychological explanations which have been attempted, such as ambition, jealousy, or aggressiveness, or the wish to create a stir, become superfluous. They are replaced by a third world situational analysis. Similarly it becomes superfluous to criticize Galileo for "dogmatism" because he stuck to the circular movement, or to introduce the idea of mysterious psychological attraction in the "mysterious circular movement."[23]

The reconstruction reflects Popper's situation not Galileo's. Historical reconstructions are not in the same relationship to evidence as are other hypotheses about the world. The historical reconstruction supports neither Popper's third world ontology nor his realism. Popper's situational analysis does not overcome the historicist dilemmas concerning representation of the past and the role of the present. Popper does think that reconstructions are objective knowledge, just like all science, produced through the method of conjectures and refutations. He objects, therefore, to the rigid distinction between the sciences and humanities and suggests that: "The method of problem solving, the method of conjectures and refutations is practised by both. It is practised in reconstructing a damaged text as well as in constructing a theory of radioactivity."[24]

For Popper, problem solving by conjecture is the universal vantage point and standard of rationality for all times and places.

But Popper defends that conclusion, as in the case of Galileo, with an historical argument. Theories are only understood by reconstruction, and knowledge is only understood retrospectively. Thus, hypotheses about historical situations reflect the standards of the present – what has succeeded in the present to solve problems and thus has emerged in the evolution of conjectures and refutations.

Popper is aware of the fallacy behind simply projecting our present assumptions into the past and, therefore, he suggests that it is precisely in our ability to criticize and reject different rational reconstructions that allows us to escape the prison-house of our own present perspective. Popper argues that we are not prisoners of frameworks, as the historicist argues, because we can criticize and reject them. Then the entire issue is whether Popper can give some basis for judging the different frameworks or versions of rationality in history. In simply holding to our current logic of problem solving Popper has not given a reason for the superiority of that "version," except that it is the present standard. Popper's reconstructions are theories about theories. Do we judge such metatheories by truth and correspondence or by utility and fruitfulness?

Popper wisely separates questions about reconstructions from questions about the actual theory being studied. Reconstruction is a metaproblem, it is a problem of understanding. This point, though perhaps labored, is crucial. If the distinction between levels were ignored, historical reconstructions would not be able to diverge from questions concerning the facts of the original problem. Two different histories could agree, for example, on the facts of Galileo's original theory of tides and that the theory itself was wrong, while disagreeing on a reconstructive explanation for the theory and the reasons behind Galileo's error. If, however, all these possible historical plots (each compatible with the historical evidence) are, for Popper, in the third world, then how do we select between the alternatives? It now is apparent that the third-world argument solves nothing. The argument only shows that past theories have logical implications and content, only some of which are apparent to us. The question of which reconstruction of the past to choose either returns us to conventional agreement in the present or to past traditions and controversies. The ultimate argument that they must converge on "the search for truth" simply will not help. The truth, as Goodman puts it, is not a strict standard of exclusion but "a docile and obedient servant."[25] Popper, in his critical and sceptical moments, admits that all history of science is simply the history of problem situations. These historically situated conjectures cannot provide evidence of progress apart from the traditions in which they reside and the contexts which, according to Popper, they reflect.

Popper's entire argument then rests on a historicist claim that his method of problem solving and rationality has emerged teleologically in history culminating in the present. The story of science is thus a "rational" story in which culture and psychology have little importance. But such a plot is not discovered in history, like a lost letter, it is constructed, normatively and regulatively, on the basis of a theory of knowledge and theory of history. Popper's theoretical assumptions are a tradition.

Consider, for example, the quote in which Popper says: "The historian's task is, therefore, so to reconstruct the problem situation as it appeared to the agent, that the actions of the agent become *adequate* to the situation."[26] The reconstruction does not simply describe actions, but aims to make the actions understandable. Understanding means an account "adequate to us." What the historical participant who is being studied once found adequate is dismissed as psychological or cultural. But the historical participant's standards are not given a fair hearing since they are dismissed for not having survived, by the natural selection of conjectures and refutations, into the present. As can now been seen, the reconstruction assumes that the distinction between psychological and rational in the third-world sense is fixed simply by adopting the present as the unchanging reference point. I am not suggesting that Popper could fix such a distinction by some other argument. The point is that the best that rational reconstruction can provide is a provisional and perspectival understanding.

I will consider in the next chapter whether there is a different argument for rationality that could, in effect, counter the historicist scepticism about philosophy and knowledge that seems to have risen like a repressed content in Popper's own reflections. There has recently been a renewed interest in what are called transcendental arguments against scepticism and relativism. In part, this reinterest was motivated by Popper's argument that inquiry must always presuppose reason and by the paradoxes Foucault finds in defenses of reference and realism external to a system of knowledge. Transcendental arguments accept that knowledge is only possible within the limits of human understanding and thus the problem of understanding is regulative of inquiry rather than a testable hypothesis. If a transcendental strategy can be defended it would establish certain limits to the historical or cultural change in knowledge.

7

Transcendental Turn

Contemporary epistemology has recently seen a revival of relativist and sceptical accounts precisely because of the wholistic arguments characteristic of the conceptual scheme approach, as discussed in Chapter 3. Doubts about reference (or what Quine calls the "inscrutability of reference") and traditional realist or empiricist theories of knowledge have, as Popper feared, encouraged subjectivist or relativist philosophical tendencies. Historicism is a version of these sentiments since it views the various conceptual schemes as so many "expressions" of the world and rejects, on relativist grounds, any "representational" account of knowledge. But in place of the confident realism of past historicists, such as Leopold Von Ranke who held that all ages are *unmittelbar zu Gott* (immediate before God), modern historicism suggests no ultimate reference or "court of appeals" by which the diverse objective worlds can be reconciled or judged. Are such doubts – about whether different theories refer to the same world or whether there is radical historical change in concepts – intelligible?

Foucault refers to "the foreign spectator in an unknown country, and the man born blind restored to light" as the two epistemological images of the eighteenth century.[1] A version of the "foreign spectator" has emerged as contemporary philosophy's thought experiment. Sometimes called the study of "alien belief systems" or "radical interpretation" it asks, for example, how anthropology succeeds in describing another culture. How do the anthropologist and the native communicate or even know if they failed to communicate? It is possible to comprehend and translate alien beliefs into "our" way of thinking?

The "foreign spectator" quandary is generated when one wonders whether a belief system somehow stands between communicators and the reference of their expressions. Not surprisingly there has been a revival of idealism in modern philosophy concerning how objectivity depends on concepts. In an aptly titled defense of realism, *One World and Our Knowledge of It*, Jay Rosenberg summarizes what he considers a neo-Hegelian treatment of the problem of representation that has been revived in recent theories of knowledge. The position he wishes to reject is that:

> We cannot hold up our representations alongside the world and thereby assess their adequacy *to* it, their correctness or incorrectness, for *all* our ostensible commerce with that world is mediated by representations. At best, we could compare our representations only with one another. We cannot compare them with the world. And, if this is so, the challenge runs, we cannot compare them in point of adequacy *to* that world. Our basis of comparison must be something else, something *internal* to the systems of representations themselves. But nothing internal to such a system of representations can bear upon its adequacy to something external to it – and the world which realism posits is just such an external something.[2]

Rosenberg argues that the correctness of systems of knowledge then resides for this approach not in the world but in the community of investigators.[3] Rosenberg hopes to show that this problem about alien beliefs is sophistic. This form of relativism asks if the standards of realism and reference change and alter within systems of concepts. But such a doubt arises because alien systems of thought are actually entertained and considered. By showing that there are such radical changes in thought, scepticism is doing what it says is impossible; it translates or represents a radically different scheme in our concepts.

To understand the problem of alien beliefs I will use, as an example, this marvellous tale of translation in the first chapter of Claude Levi-Strauss's *The Savage Mind*.⁴ The anthropologist, E. Smith Bowen, recounts her difficulties in learning an African tribal language. Her informants, considering what would be for them the most elementary level of instruction, used plant identification as their beginning point. They collected a large number of specimens and told Smith Bowen the name of each plant as they showed her that plant. But since she could not identify the plants to begin with, her progress was shockingly slow. She says: "My instructors could not realize that it was not the words but the plants which baffled me."

Smith Bowen assumes that her linguistic confusion was due to her ignorance of botany. Armed with a comparable system of botanical classification or identification from her own culture, she believes she would not have been confused by the language lessons. The difference between the tribe and herself was a mere matter of priorities and information. The natives chose plants as prime teaching examples because plants are vital to their lives. That, in fact, explains their detailed system of plant classification. In the same teaching situation, we might choose different objects, typical of our own interests (perhaps the famous pens, tables, and chairs so loved by philosophers). Thus, any difficulties in understanding other peoples are matters of pedagogy not ontology. Translation occasions only trivial problems, Smith Bowen argues, as long as a common classification system is in place. It is questions about the existence of some common agreement which raises radical doubts about our understanding alien systems of thought.

Levi-Strauss argues at length about the deeper implications of Smith Bowen's confusion. If native classifications are not mere rationales for a natural utility, as Levi-Strauss tries to show, then classifications reveal or make possible the utility of knowledge, not the reverse. Primitive classification is a cognitive enterprise (as the title of Levi-Strauss's book is meant to convey). Therefore, neither appealing to our own classifications nor to some assumption about what is naturally "useful" in all cultures resolves radical questions of translation. Smith Bowen assumes the distinction between "plants" and "words" and then locates her confusion within that distinction. The very distinction of word and object is in question. A residual uncertainty remains which no amount of finger pointing can resolve. The anthropologist and the native handle "things," but she does not comprehend the system which defines and circumscribes "object." Learning another system of thought raises ontological questions.

The Savage Mind argues that common sense, which assumes that a single classification is manifested in reality, treats alien belief systems as the result of some distortion or ideology. Primitive thought was not studied as a cognitive system, according to Levi-Strauss, because it was thought by anthropologists to be only a pretense for the purposes of trade, kinship, or mythology. For Levi-Strauss, however, this emphasis on utility and ideology is a cultural bias on the part of modern thought.

> This thirst for objective knowledge is one of the most neglected aspects of the thought of people we call "primitive." Even if it is rarely directed towards facts at the same level as those with which modern science is concerned, it implies comparable intellectual applications and methods of observation. In both cases the universe is an object of thought at least as much as it is a means of satisfying needs.
>
> Every civilization tends to overestimate the objective orientation of its thought and this tendency is never absent.[5]

The last sentence shifts doubt to "our" system in cases of radical interpretation. Levi-Strauss is not a relativist and defends a realist view of science throughout *The Savage Mind*, even attacking historicism in a famous criticism of Sartre. But he uses this sceptical and historicist strategy to dislodge what he considers an unexamined bias against primitive thought.

While Levi-Strauss's strategy saves "primitive" thought from ethnocentric bias, he pays a price for this generosity. After cataloguing an amusing list of medicinal aides and cures characteristic of traditional cultures Levi-Strauss concludes that the purpose of classification is not practical.

> It meets intellectual requirements rather than or instead of satisfying needs.
>
> The real question is not whether the touch of a

woodpecker's beak does in fact cure a toothache. It is rather whether there is a point of view from which a woodpecker's beak and a man's tooth can be seen as "going together" (the use of congruity for therapeutic purposes being only one of its possible uses), and whether some initial order can be introduced into the universe by means of these groupings.[6]

Things can "go together" in endless variations, none are privileged and all are useful. But while I may agree that primitive thought is not entirely ideological, are there not errors? Woodpecker's beak, for instance, does not cure a toothache. Of course, further investigation may reveal a chemical found in the beaks of certain species that dulls pain. But that would be a triumph for "our" system. It would grant cognitive respectability to traditional thought only under the hegemony of modern science. Am I foregoing criticism of traditional thought or actually proving the superiority of modernism?

Levi-Strauss claims that traditional thought and modern science are parallel and autonomous modes of knowledge. What Levi-Strauss ignores is the historicist implication that giving traditional thought autonomy, and its own criteria of utility, relativizes modern thought since a culture's cognitive strategies can only be judged internally. Can Levi-Strauss reconcile this epistemology of radical interpretation with scientific realism?

The most optimistic answer, compatible with Levi-Strauss's realist side, is that traditional thought is the product of the same concept elaboration as modern science. Levi-Strauss's distinction between the "savage" and modern mind concerns only what is *given*, but the conceptual operations are the same. Modern and traditional thought are both elaborate conceptual schemes and it is neither puzzling nor surprising that the schemes are diverse. Nature does not guide theorizing; objects do not come stamped with appropriate classifications.

Robin Horton develops Levi-Strauss's insight through an epistemological account of traditional thought using Popper's methodology.[7] Horton agrees with Levi-Strauss that traditional thought is cognitive, but also agrees with common sense that it fails to produce knowledge. Its failure, however, is not due to its wild speculations or bizarre classifications. Traditional thought represents what Horton calls a "closed predicament." He means that in traditional cultures the cognitive scheme and the social system are entwined. Since attacks on concepts become attacks on social practices, traditional thought restricts criticism. As E.E. Evans-Pritchard demonstrated, the Azande protect their belief in magic by elaborate social strategies and taboos against theoretical challenge.[8] Tribal members are blocked from questioning the predictive failures or inconsistencies in shamanist practice. Thus the concept elaboration in traditional societies is artificially or sociologically restricted by linking knowledge or inquiry concerning procreation, weather, or medicine to social customs and practices.

The "open predicament" characteristic of modern society according to Horton, treats science as autonomous from social life and thus frees it for inquiry and criticism. Horton's point is that modern thought is like traditional thought in its speculation or positing of entities, but differs from it in its critical strategies. Of course, there were and will continue to be exceptions. The Lysenko affair in the Soviet Union (in which the study of genetics was prohibited and condemned as a "bourgeois science") and continuing efforts by religious groups to restrict teaching evolution are based on fears that theoretical innovation subverts social practices. But these controversies are explicit and thus distinct from the resistance found in traditional closed predicaments where the very question of conceptual change cannot arise.

In primitive (or what Horton calls traditional) societies, the entire social structure is built around preserving and conserving the total belief system against transgression. Thus, in the second part of his article Horton suggests factors such as navigation and the invention of writing which accelerated the erosion of traditional hegemony. Writing, for example, fixed the fleeting formulations of oral teachings, making possible such critical procedures as comparison, consistency, testing, and exegesis (the discovery of logic and rhetoric). Contact with other cultures, simultaneously, relativized social practices. The discovery of convention, not nature, lies at the base of the Western scientific tradition. The open predicament is not wedded to any particular speculation or entity, no matter how theoretically successful or socially useful.

The "foreign spectator" experiment, however, is another case in which Popperian self-criticism turns into scepticism. The anthropologist-translator wonders whether she has correctly understood another scheme. Wonder, which can be a spur to innovation, can also be a nagging doubt. The "outsider" suspends her beliefs in order to understand alien beliefs. But the ensuing doubt is not reciprocal. The native may find the anthropologist strange or childlike, especially if the anthropologist lacks, as did Smith Bowen, certain native competences. Confronting the "other," however, does not weaken the native's belief system, as Horton explains. In fact, the presence of the "other" reifies those beliefs, at least initially. It is the spectator alone who wonders if understanding is possible and how beliefs get "fixed." Perhaps, she fears, beliefs are fixed apart from what the world is like.

But Horton offers a way out of radical scepticism since the difference between "open" and "closed" rests on the reaction to falsifying evidence. If a tradition resists falsification then there should be a sociological or external explanation of its failure to produce knowledge. It is not necessary to get "inside" another culture and try to judge the strangeness of its concepts by context. Rationality and concept elaboration are everywhere the same.

But this whole solution rests on the argument that resistance towards falsification is the sign of the unscientific and thus builds on the distinction between external and internal explanations. Popperian conventionalism is the rule always to accept counterevidence. But experience alone cannot provide counterevidence. Counterevidence requires another theory. Should I take the success of the Azande shaman as a falsification of modern medicine? Would I be unscientific if I didn't? Since the Azande have procedures for dealing with failures of magic, is there some rule which specifies that they be persuaded that modern accounts have better procedures?

Horton's solution works by holding that there is a "neutral" strategy for interpreting cognitive schemes (a scientific method). But interpretation should proceed without simply assuming the common denominator of modern science. Perhaps the problem rests, then, not in finding the right method but in the presupposition of a dualism of scheme and experience, or of internal and external – a presupposition held by Horton and others who unsuccessfully try to discuss how concepts "fit" or "match" the world.

In "On the Notion of a Conceptual Scheme," Donald Davidson tries to remove the relativist scandal from the idea of a conceptual scheme without determining which schemes are scientific and which are not.[9] Instead, Davidson attacks the metaphor itself: the notion of a "grid" over against an "outside" which filters through. It is the persistence of this family of metaphors that creates a dilemma about interpretation.

For Davidson, the question being asked is: "Do . . . two people have different conceptual schemes if they speak languages that fail of intertranslatibility?" We detect schemes by translation failures, as Smith Bowen did. In such cases, there are only two possibilities; either translations completely fail or only partially succeed.

Smith Bowen and the African tribe that used plants for language instruction may have been only "words," not "worlds" apart. But can that question be settled by words alone? Can being worlds apart be communicated or interpreted in language? Davidson properly merges the problem of alien belief systems with the larger study of interpretation and demands an interpretive strategy that "makes no assumptions about shared meanings, concepts or beliefs."

An example of such an interpretive strategy occurs in Dan Sperber's *Rethinking Symbolism*, where he discusses how to distinguish error and symbolism in traditional thought. In his work among the Droze of southern Ethiopia he developed a selective ear for listening to information. As the practice of cultivation was discussed he barely paid attention, but as soon as the respondent explained how the head of the household must sow the grain for a good harvest Sperber took note. Only when illness was attributed to an evil eye, Sperber admits, did he have anything significant to work with.

Sperber argues that in distinguishing between error and symbolism an interpretive strategy should be conservative toward the native belief system.

A Droze friend says to me that pregnancy lasts nine months, I think, "Good, they know that." When he adds, "but in some clans it lasts eight or ten months," I think, "That's symbolic." Why? Because it is false. This needs clarification. Not all errors immediately strike me as symbolic, nor all symbolic discourse as necessarily erroneous. . . . The economics of error does not differ essentially from that of valid inference. Both try to account for a maximum of data by means of a minimum of hypotheses, and are capable of being falsified; . . . symbolic discourse, on the contrary, ignores this economics; it only retains from experience a minimum of fragments to establish a maximum of hypotheses, without caring to put them to the test; . . . I note then as symbolic all activity where the means put into play seem to me to be clearly disproportionate to the explicit or implicit end, whether this end be knowledge, communication or production – that is to say, all activity whose rationale escapes me.[10]

Sperber's approach does not treat all resistance to tests as a sign of error. Symbolism allows for a broader cognitive system than science. But Sperber's strategy detects symbolism by "all activity whose rationale escapes me" and, clearly, that phrase begs the central question of radically different schemes.

Davidson, like Sperber, holds the "charitable" approach to interpretation which assumes from the start that beliefs are normal and our interpretation should always preserve consistency. It would violate the principle of charity to interpret everyday conversation by assuming fellow humans were paranoid schizophrenics, though such an intepretation would "succeed." The cost of such explanations is in the economy of charitable assumptions. But Davidson's defense of such strategies is not just over the economy of assumptions. Only *after* a charitable interpretation, Davidson argues, is any meaningful disagreement possible because the detection of error, like symbolism, requires common assumptions.

Translating traditional thought, or any radically different scheme, is a decision on how to apply the "principle of charity." The precise question is whether there are "scheme neutral" guidelines on where to accommodate (that is, take differences as symbolic or erroneous) and where to plead the presence of a scheme so radically different that perhaps our categories do not apply. Can any argument specify in advance where charitable differences leave off and radical intranslatibility begins? Though Davidson grants he cannot settle disagreements in advance, he does argue that he can, in advance, separate meaningful for meaningless dispute.

> The method [or radical translation] is not designed to eliminate disagreement, nor can it; its purpose is to make meaningful disagreement possible and thus depends entirely on a foundation – some foundation – in agreement.[11]

Arguing in this way, Davidson tries to show that the relativist scandal is an illusion. A total failure of translation would mean that there is a conceptual scheme fitting the world, maybe true of the world, but without any interpretation and translation. Since that possibility divorces truth claims about the world from their intepretation or translation, it simultaneously condemns all efforts to detect such a scheme. Thus total failure of translation is a Pickwickian danger.

But the remaining partial failures in translation, he holds, yield no theoretical scandal. Since there is no external rule (following the sense of the metaphor) for distinguishing between charitable and radical strategies of translation, no dramatic conclusion follows from the normal partial failures of understanding – given that total failures of understanding are unintelligible. Difficulties in interpretation provide evidence neither for nor against relativistic historicism. Rather than continue the search for a common denominator, or proclaim the truth of relativism, Davidson offers the therapeutic suggestion of abandoning the conceptual scheme metaphor that caused all the confusion in the first place.

> Neither a fixed stock of meanings nor a theory-neutral reality, can provide . . . a ground for comparison of conceptual schemes. It would be a mistake to look further for such a ground if by that we mean something

conceived as common to incommensurable schemes. In abandoning the search, we abandon the attempt to make sense of the metaphor of a single space within which each scheme has a position and provides a point of view.[12]

Davidson's strategy is verificationist. The notion of a total failure in translation cannot be made intelligible because it cannot be detected. A case of radical incommensurability can not be "pointed out" without thereby using an inconsistent argument. Thus Davidson treats arguments for radical incommensurability as "self-excepting" arguments, just as Plato treated sophistic relativism.

But Davidson also knows that more sophisticated versions of "reality is relative to a scheme," or accounts of the "historical captivity" of philosophy, are always possible and, therefore, he wants to dismiss the whole notion of conceptual schemes. Such an argument would have the added benefit of not only removing the relativist scandal, but preventing further sceptical mischief with the partial failures in translation which Davidson's account admits. If, Davidson argues, no sense can be made of an unintelligible "outside" which is yet the object of all attempts at presentation, then, by dismissing this Kantian division between schemes and an inaccessible reality, we are simply left with reality itself.

> In giving up the dualism of scheme and world we do not give up the world, but re-establish unmediated touch with familiar objects whose antics make our sentences and opinions true or false.[13]

Davidson's final stance denies any mediation between the knower and the known, short of an immediate state of affairs in which we "re-establish touch" with objects. Of course, this position ends any relativist or historicist attempts to move from the underdetermination of reality on theory to a "truth is relative to a scheme" conclusion. But the cost of Davidson's defense is to reintroduce, in that single sentence conclusion, direct acquaintance with the world – what Hegel called "immediacy" between subject and object. It was precisely criticism of knowledge by direct acquaintance which originally sparked historicist and relativist epistemologies in contemporary philosophy.

Direct acquaintance accounts of knowledge, no matter how sophisticated, clash with the growth and evolution of knowledge. From the viewpoint that knowledge manifests itself through the "antics" of objects, the history of cognition must be treated as a dull, massive delusion in which failed attempts at knowledge are explained by sociological forces of distortion or blindness. In other words, direct acquaintance begins with "transparency" and is then forced to introduce endless epicycles to explain obscurity and the failure of a direct contact with reality. If knowledge comes at once and all in a piece, only some hidden perversity or ideology can explain why traditions fail simply to see the "antics" of "familiar objects." Hence, Davidson continues (in spite of his criticism of the metaphor) the external-internal division in epistemology, and thus the need for a sociology of knowledge. A theory of ideology becomes necessary because to reintroduce immediacy or direct acquaintance simultaneously creates the need for an account of failures to acquire knowledge in the past.

Historicism, for instance, does relativize both "antics" and "familiar objects" to a context and tradition, rejecting all essentialist and naturalist accounts, and also the fixed distinction between that which is internal and external in knowledge. Davidson does not necessarily object to such relativity, as it expresses itself in the practical problems of interpretation. However, in rejecting the dualism of scheme and the world in a logical fashion and thus escaping scepticism, Davidson leans on the myth of the given.

If Davidson's conclusion of a re-established touch with reality is separated from the rest of the article there is a different thrust to his position. All of acts of translation or interpretation succeed "in a way" and for a purpose or interest, but not absolutely and definitively. Stuck with the continual threat of partial failures, one conclusion is to deny that the world is manifest or knowledge transparent. All interpretations are provisional. Such a version need not, as Davidson shows, hold to some idea of radical incomprehensibility within changes of knowledge. But for purposes of critical flexibility, expressions of knowledge cannot be identified with the world as it really is.

I have argued that Davidson is holding a "direct acquaintance" view of knowledge in his attack on the notion of conceptual schemes. In a recent study, *The Refutation of Scepticism*, A.C. Grayling interprets Davidson as making a transcendental argument against conceptual scheme relativism or scepticism.[14] This interesting reading of Davidson directs attention to a form of argument implicit in Popper, that the human senses are theoretical hypotheses about the world; or in analyses of the history of science as the history of conceptual presuppositions that make knowledge possible, as found in Conant or Kuhn. Can the problem of historicism be resolved by a transcendental strategy?

The transcendental argument was crafted by Kant in his clever but controversial reply to Hume's scepticism. Kant did not try to answer scepticism by securing some access to the world such that our "impressions" could be said to mirror the world as it really is. Rather, Kant accepted the sceptical position that our impressions or sensations do *not* tell us what the world is *really* like. By granting this crucial assumption – i.e. that all knowledge is knowledge of appearances – Kant tried to show that the demand for knowledge of "things as they really are" is either an impossible demand or simply supplied by normal experience. As Kant summarized his reply to Hume:

> My own labors in the *Critique of Pure Reason* were occasioned by Hume's skeptical teaching. . . . I granted that, when Hume took the objects of experience as things-in-themselves (as is almost always done), he was entirely correct in declaring the concept of cause to be deceptive and an illusion; . . . Thus he could not admit such a priori knowledge of things-in-themselves. . . . From my investigations, however, it resulted that the objects with which we have to do in experience are by no means things-in-themselves but appearances.[15]

Kant argues that the things-in-themselves are inaccessible because they contradict the way in which "experience is possible" and the way in which objects of experience are "alone knowable to us." Kant's notion of possible experience means neither logical possibility nor an empirical inquiry into the psychological or physiological bases which makes experience. The science of psychology, for instance, would simply presuppose a demonstration of the transcendental or conceptual possibility of experience.

Thus Kant admits in the phrase "alone knowable to us" a truth to scepticism, namely scepticism about the ultimate reality of our objects of knowledge. But Kant hoped to control the destructive impact of this admission by showing that these conditions for the possibility of the world as appearance are universal, a priori (prior to experience) and humanly invariant. Kant called this position "transcendental idealism" because knowledge through perception gave no access to reality understood as the ultimate thing-in-itself. Experience is constituted by "our" conceptual scheme, but such a scheme is necessary for experience.

Historicism is distantly related to the Kantian transcendental critique, because in both positions objectivity is constituted and representations of the world are treated as appearances. But, according to historicism, the world as appearance changes in the manner of a cultural convention or alterable arrangement. In place of Kant's argument that there are necessary categories, historicism offers nothing more than relative and internal justification. Could a modern argument similar to Kant's show necessary limits to the historical diversity that generated the historicist tendency in philosophy? If so, there would be a reply to the kind of relativism of conceptual schemes implied by Strawson's claim that: "It is possible to describe types of experience very different from the experience we actually have."[16]

The argument is that a necessary conceptual/perceptual scheme, making experience possible, transcends cultural and historical context. The possibility of knowledge is not historically conditioned: on the contrary, what makes knowledge possible makes the idea of historicity possible. To imagine in history different frameworks of knowledge or objectivities of experience, as Foucault does for example, must already assume a common precondition. Hence radical conceptual change or "epistemological breaks" are impossible. For these reasons, Grayling considers a modern transcendental argument the only viable philosophical reply to pernicious scepticism and relativism.

> What is typical of transcendental arguments proper is that they purport to establish the conditions necessary for experience, or experience of a certain kind, *as a whole*; and, at their most controversial, to establish a conclusion about the nature and existence of the external world . . . in consequence of paying attention to what *has* to be the case for there to be *experience*, or in order for experience to be as it is.[17]

How are universal presuppositions of experience discovered or argued for: Grayling's answer is that a transcendental strategy (which Grayling compares to Davidson's approach) shows that radical alternatives in understanding the world are unintelligible. Disagreement cannot occur at the presuppositional level, but only at an empirical level held in common for all human subjectivity. Changes in the history of knowledge, as appealed to by historicists like Kuhn, are simply over contingent matters of fact. To imagine deeper disputes about knowledge is to pose an irresolvable historical question. The point is, for Grayling, that changes in the history of knowledge raise no radical or fundamental doubts.

> In short, then, sceptical doubt is shown to be idle or pointless because the beliefs the sceptic asks us to justify turn out to be necessary to our thought and talk of the world, and nothing counts as thought and talk unless it is recognisable as such from the standpoint of the thought and talk we enjoy; so that the beliefs to which we are committed, and to which essential reference must be made for any explanation or description of experience in general, are simply not negotiable, that is, are not open to doubt.[18]

Grayling holds that foundational beliefs in perception and the concept of an object are not mere "choices" or cultural conventions, but that which we are "absolutely bound to believe." In other words, the concept of perceptions of independently existing objects which can be identified and reidentified is a necessary condition of all knowledge and historical controversy, not an option that changes in history. These fundamental beliefs transcend or are presupposed by all meaningful historical or theoretical debate. Meaningful discourse presupposes objects identified and individualized in a consistent and systematic fashion. As Jürgen Habermas puts it, "non-objectivatable perceptions would be a contradiction in terms. They would not be perceptions but figments of imagination, illusions, phantasms, etc."[19]

Grayling stresses that he is not a realist. These presupposed concepts are not what is "really real" nor are they the theoretical objects of a particular science. Grayling's transcendentalism concerns minimal presuppositions of "objecthood" or "personhood," neutral between competitive scientific theories and theories of knowledge. All that the argument shows is that belief in objects "is a *presupposition* of our thinking, talking, and acting as we do, such that to doubt it *is* a presupposition is not to do something merely false, but senseless."[20]

Grayling insists that the possibility of "other representations of the world" is finally empty since he has shown that all "recognitional capacity" must be grounded or explained on the possession or employment of "the belief in the existence of objects." Grayling's defense of this claim is modest. He admits that Kant's attempt to deduce necessary categories is a fruitless effort and that it would violate our current view that all knowledge claims are fallible. Grayling's demonstration of scepticism's incoherence is based on reconstructing, retrospectively, any theoretical debate in such a way as to maintain a common assumption.

Grayling's effort at that level is, therefore, not very different from historicism. Except that historicism would deny that such a reconstruction is the result of some special kind of philosophical argument, or proves that this common assumption is an a priori, universal conditions for all experience. For the historicist, a tradition has been reconstructed. Grayling's reply is that even the possibility of multiple reconstructions must presuppose the same minimal concepts of objects and persons. But Grayling's victory over scepticism requires more than the possibility of interpreting such theoretical debates as commensurable. He must show, without using Kant's stronger argument concerning the transcendental deduction of categories, that only the commensurable interpretations are meaningful. Historicism does not deny that such interpretations are possible. But is there a special philosophical investigation of concepts that could in advance set the limits of epistemological traditions?

Jürgen Habermas has, like Grayling, defended the autonomy of philosophy against historicist arguments and what Habermas calls scientism through a transcendental strategy. But, unlike Grayling, Habermas has recently questioned the efficacy of such arguments, as I will discuss below.

Habermas's account of the transcendental defense begins with his reconstruction of epistemology from Hegel to Marx. According to Habermas, Hegel's criticism of Kant revealed an important problem of epistemology. Hegel, in an argument similar to Davidson's rejection of the separation between concept and content, wished to show that Kant's separation of our access to knowledge from reality encouraged sceptical and relativist conclusions. But Hegel's attack on Kant's escape from scepticism, Habermas continues, had to assume the possibility of absolute knowledge, precisely what Kant denied. Even given the assumption of absolute knowledge, however, Hegel analyzed knowledge claims *retrospectively*. Only from some final vantage point will there be a stable meaning to the past. Thus in Hegel, there are different historical categories and manifestations of experience. Habermas agrees that Hegel's philosophical project of a final totalization or "ultimate reference" is not salvageable because "we cannot even meaningfully talk of knowledge without identifying the conditions of possible knowledge."[21] He emphasizes Kant's "verificationist" argument that an absolute vantage point for knowledge is unintelligible, because going beyond the limits of human experience produces irresolvable dilemmas.

But Hegel's attack on Kant is not entirely discredited. In Habermas's view, Hegel showed that Kant's epistemology rested upon hidden cultural or historical presuppositions. The first is Kant's commitment to the "sure march of science" and the privilege Kant gives to the natural sciences as a source for knowledge of the world. Kant demands that philosophy begin with and account for the superiority of science over all competitive accounts of nature. But Hegel, as a critic of the Enlightenment, relativizes scientific success and progress to one among many historical *expressions* of Spirit, with no privileged status. Thus Hegel's "phenomenological" approach to all acts of knowledge suspends ontological assumptions and commitments and reconstructs the context, development, and internal justification of each form of understanding. Hegel considers this suspension or destruction of assumptions as the consistent development of phenomenalism. Philosophy can express the ultimate totality of experience, but knowledge cannot represent the world directly without the mediation of history and conceptual change.

The second cultural or historical presupposition Hegel finds in Kant is the conception of a knowing subject. Hegel argues that this subjectivity is actually a product of historical development and culture. Modern subjectivity is constructed, not given, in experience; the foundational concept of the individual is historical. Thus Hegel argues that apart from some final perspective on the world, there is no way to demonstrate that the assumptions of a particular culture or subjectivity are universal. Habermas considers these Hegelian arguments crucial to understanding the crisis of modern epistemology which distrusts the objectivity of the "present" and whatever appears as natural or given.

For Habermas, Hegel had raised the possibility that "the transcendental relation between subject and object alters itself behind its back." Even though modern philosophy rejects Hegel's project of absolute knowledge, it remains, like Hegel, suspicious of universal standards.

In Habermas' version of intellectual history, Marx momentarily closed the issue by having knowledge constituted by human activity or practice rather than sensation. In Marx, humanity's constant relation to nature through labor constitutes what Habermas calls "the historically alterable inventory of societies." Marx's concept of labor is philosophical rather than economic or political. Marx is a neo-Kantian who attempts to show that labor establishes an invariant relationship of human beings to the world and the possibility of knowledge through this constant of human activity. Marxism, like pragmatism, tried to transcend philosophical debates – the Kantian "antinomies" of speculation about reality – through practical activity transforming reality, rather than through pure philosophical argument.

Labor, though an historically variable activity, carries with it a "transcendental necessity" that binds together the objectivity of nature and the human interest to control nature. Habermas calls such a position a transcendental argument on the necessity of *intervention* for knowledge of an objective world.

> The objectivity of the possible objects of experience is constituted within a conceptual-perceptual scheme rooted in deep-seated structures of human action; this scheme is equally binding on all subject that keep alive through labor. The objectivity of the possible objects of experience is thus grounded in the identity of a natural substratum, namely the bodily organization of man, which is oriented toward action, and not in an original unity of apperception, which, according to Kant, guarantees with transcendental necessity the identity of an ahistorical consciousness in general.[22]

Habermas conceives of labor, therefore, as what he calls a "cognitive transcendental interest," rather than an empirical or psychological fact of humanity. While Habermas agrees, in general, with Marx's strategy of replying to historical relativism through a practical account of human intelligibility, he does not accept that labor alone provides such objectivity. Habermas does not believe that representation as a project of understanding should be collapsed entirely into practical intervention. The mistake of pragmatism or Marxism, in his view, is that instrumental control of nature is not applicable, as a transcendental interest, to understanding the symbolic system of a culture. The world can be represented in both ways and the rules or conventions behind symbols, unlike the rules for representing the world as an object of instrumental control, change in human history and are not guided by utility.

Human knowledge, for Habermas, is based on a distinction between sensory experience (observation of the natural world) and communicative experience (understanding of culture and history). The two orientations constitute two distinct "object-spheres." But this distinction is not itself an expression of cultural convention. It reflects the two possible human objectivities of control or interpretation, a difference corresponding to the distinction between the social and natural sciences.

Science alone cannot produce knowledge and requires philo-sophical reflection and criticism. It is by philosophical reflection that we grasp the constitutive interests of knowledge. When the human subject is engaged in the world it proceeds with its given categories. Only in reflective criticism does subjectivity disengage from the world and free itself from immediate conditions. Critical self-reflection reveals that reason is interested. But in his early work, *Knowledge and Human Interests*, Habermas does not want this "interestedness" of reason to end up supporting some historicist relativism about knowledge. He stresses, therefore, the transcendental strategy.

> Empirical analytic science discloses reality . . . as . . . instrumental action. In accordance with their immanent meaning, nomological statements . . . *grasp reality with regard to technical control that, under specified conditions, is possible everywhere and at all times.* The hermeneutic sciences do not disclose reality under a different transcendental framework. Rather, they are directed toward the transcendental structure of various actual forms of life. . . . *they grasp interpretations of reality with regard to possible . . . mutual understanding specific to a given hermeneutic starting point.*[23]

Thus, for Habermas, historicism confuses these "subjective," transcendental conditions of objectivity with the empirical dis-covery of historical conditions. Philosophical reflection on categories is neither an empirical inquiry nor a debate about the content of knowledge. Historicism does understand that disputes in knowledge can occur at the level of "forms of life," the presuppositions of experience that precede empirical inquiry. But historicism mistakenly reduces these reflective disputes to something relative, conventional, and arbitrary. Rather, Habermas argues, there is a conceptual necessity to the world as we experience it in all historical contexts; there can be no sense to the notion of many worlds. Precisely in philosophical reflection, historical "prejudice" is revealed as possible only because there is a single possible objectivity of culture prior to the historical capture of ideas. Philosophy is autonomous.

For example, Habermas criticizes Herbert Marcuse for treating the rationality of science as "historically derived and therefore a transitory a priori structure."[24] Habermas thus characterizes Marcuse as using an historicist approach to reduce science to an "historically unique project." Habermas concludes that if scientific knowledge is treated as just an historical project – that is, not based on a necessary rather than transitory constitution of the world as a possible object of knowledge – then alternative objectifications of the world must be possible. But Habermas holds that such alternative objectifications are "not conceivable." A world objectified without the transcendental interests of control and interpretation can neither be conceptualized nor known. Marcuse has not understood, according to Habermas, that scientific objectivity is different from the relativity of symbols found in cultural studies. There are not various different natures as there are different cultures. The universal interest for technical control makes knowledge of nature possible independently of cultural meanings and symbolization. Habermas insists that we distinguish between projects of symbolic interaction and what he calls "purposive-rational action."

> This means, however, that the two projects are projec-
> tions of work and language, i.e. projects of the human
> species as a whole and not of an individual epoch, a
> specific class, or a surpassable situation. The idea of a
> New Science will not stand up to logical scrutiny any
> more than that of a New Technology, if indeed science
> is to remain the meaning of modern science inherently
> oriented to possible technical control. For this function,
> as for scientific-technical progress in general, there is no
> more "humane" substitute.[25]

Knowledge of history is also possible because of the constitution of a different object-sphere. The possible object-spheres are limited prior to experience and, therefore, historical diversity does not limit the social sciences. The difference between the world constituted as an object of technical control as against an object of communicative understanding is a matter of transcendental possibility, not historical investigation.

Habermas, like Davidson, wants to show that radical incommensurability is unintelligible. He also, however, rejects a realist view that scientific knowledge represents the world as it is and the idea of some direct acquaintance with states of affairs in the world. Scientific studies, for Habermas, are limited to instrumental success. For that reason Habermas's opposition to historicism is based not on realism, but a modified transcendental argument for objectivity.

Habermas has, however, recently qualified his early commitment to a transcendental analysis in *Knowledge in Human Interests* with the "Postscript" to the book's reedition and in an article "What is Universal Pragmatics?" In the "Postscript," Habermas does continue to describe his position as a "new and transformed transcendental philosophy." Habermas's modification of Kant mainly consists in his joining the transcendental reply to scepticism with fallibilism in science. Habermas distinguishes, for that reason, arguments concerning what makes objectivity possible (transcendental arguments) from debates about the truth of some specific claim (fallible arguments). There can never be certainty about the correct representation of experience, even though objectivity in experience rests on a priori interests. In showing that there are conceptual presuppositions for objectivity, one cannot thereby determine which scientific theory is true; "this *objectivity* of stated experience is not the same as the truth of a statement."[26]

To the extent that this admission weakens the transcendental refutation of scepticism it also strengthens the reason for historicism Habermas tried to prevent such a conclusion by stressing that theoretical disagreements can only concern the interpretation of an objectivity which is already constituted universally and prior to the empirical level, in which claims are treated as fallible. The existence of such disagreements does not lead to any philosophical doubts, within the limits of human experience, about objectivity or reference.

> But as long as we are not angels or animals, these languages cannot *transform* the structures themselves into conditions of another object domain. It is always the experience of identical objects of *our* world which is being interpreted differently according to the state of scientific progress we happen to have reached.[27]

Habermas carves out a position which lies between emphasis on historical change in object spheres and realism. Access to "our world which is being interpreted" is possible and objective because there are domains of instrumentality and symbolism. These object domains are not true or false – though once constituted, empirical claims about them can be discussed and defended. The question of whether an object domain is true or not is wrongly formulated.

But given that position, Habermas cannot contrast interpretation with "our world." What content can be given to "our world" such that a special philosophical argument, different from argument within the sciences, could establish universal conditions for knowledge about it?

In the later article, "What is Universal Pragmatics?," Habermas separates what he now calls a "universal-pragmatic reconstruction of argumentative discourse" from a transcendental analysis. Habermas concludes that transcendental arguments are simply hypotheses about what makes experience coherent. Rather than being a special philosophical argument for universality, a transcendental analysis is nothing more than a charitable interpretation. Habermas dismisses at this point any attempt to deduce or prove the validity of our concepts. He thus weakens considerably the meaning of a priori. In analyzing what categories are necessary presuppositions of experience, one is conjecturing on a possible coherence within historical and empirical experiences. Such hypotheses rest simply on "the competence of knowing subjects who judge which experience may be called coherent. . . . Every reconstruction of a basic conceptual system of possible experience has to be regarded as a hypothetical proposal."[28]

Any necessity between reason and the world – which Habermas hoped to establish in his earlier work against relativism and scepticism – is now merely a practical strategy for understanding. The point is that to treat such understanding as a hypothesis to be tested or verified is to abandon the transcendental argument. A transcendental argument concerns the condition for possible experience and cannot itself be verified or tested. The presupposition that makes it possible to test knowledge cannot itself be the object of testing. Furthermore, if evidence could unambiguously select between interpretations, then the whole sceptical problem of frameworks would have never arisen.

Habermas gives several reasons for not using transcendental analysis. First, he argues that even with transcendental arguments we cannot exclude the possibility that our concepts have *contingent boundary conditions*. This point means that concepts cannot be taken as fixed apart from internal contexts. Such a conventionalist admission raises the specter of relativism once again.

Habermas suggests that for all practical purposes we need not be concerned with such relativism, because the basic conceptual system of human beings is shaped by evolution. Habermas's recourse here to evolutionary epistemology and naturalism tries to resolve these epistemological debates through some fact of nature. Of course, the theory of evolution is itself an interpretation, not a dictate of experience. In other words, the debate is resolved not by the facts of the matter, but by a coherent conceptual scheme. But even if that limitation is ignored, by appealing to the fact that certain concepts (such as the independent existence of objects or other minds) have been useful to humans in their survival – if such epistemic utility could even be shown – this does not, in turn, demonstrate the necessity of those concepts. When confronted with another culture's treatment of selfhood or causation, the question remains whether understanding how that experience is organized, by appealing to the competence of the subjects, reveals something we all have in common. By projecting the heuristic of interpretation he recommends into the natural world, Habermas simply restricts philosophical reflection and debate. The very reasons he gave for abandoning the transcendental approach do not lend support to this belated and weak naturalistic solution.

Habermas's central and stronger argument is that while our concepts are relative, the behavioral systems of humans are invariant. But this conclusion does not, unfortunately, settle the questions that began this whole discussion. Heuristic standards such as utility, adaption, or familiarity are independent of truth. Behavioral preconditions simply lead back to an assumption that knowledge which fits the criteria of simplicity, efficacy, or human need is objective and thus universal. But this argument is too weak to stand as refutation of historical changes in conceptual schemes. If the behavior systems of humans, as product of evolutionary biology, alone make objective knowledge possible, there should be no deep theoretical disputes. But since such disputes do occur, Habermas's reply reinterprets them within the assumed heuristic that a universal pattern of human behavior lies beneath all controversies about knowledge.

Habermas's continuing quest for an answer to relativism and scepticism has recently turned to the analyses of utterances, meanings, and intentionality in language. That inquiry is what he calls universal pragmatics and would apparently provide the framework for all possible communication.[20] Habermas's new project bears a similarity to attempts by linguistic analysis and ordinary language philosophy to solve conceptual problems through a reflection on the normal usage of language. Habermas admits that with this new study of communication and language the transcendental approach "recedes into the background."

The whole distinction between a priori and empirical, or reconstructive and empirical analysis blurs – just as historicism has always argued. Kant's original distinction between the a priori and the a posteriori fails to hold if the only criteria for such demarcation are relative measures such as practical success, instrumental control, or meaningful coherence. The basic strategy behind transcendental philosophy was to discover an invariant point of view by showing that a certain objectification was necessarily presupposed by all experience. Habermas concludes that his new study of language will replace or improve the transcendental strategy.

> However, I do not find any correspondent to this idea under which the analyses of general presuppositions of communication might be carried out. . . . A transcendental investigation transposed to processes of understanding would thus have to be oriented around another model – not the epistemological model of the constitution of experience but perhaps the model of deep and surface structure.[30]

The point of this discussion has been to show why the transcendental strategy does not eliminate an historicist position about knowledge and representation. Historicism does treat the objectivity of knowledge as constituted and internally justified. The diverse historical schemes, however, can only be known partially and provisionally from the vantage point of the present. Historicism accepts the sceptical argument against certain knowledge of the past and turns to reconstructions or interpretations. Historical interpretation of systems of knowledge is possible and coherent but marked by indeterminacy over the translation of basic concepts. This fundamental "inscrutability" about versions of the world cannot, unfortunately, be removed by the philosopher's pen.

Conclusion

My presentation of these philosophical reflections on historicism has been framed by an inversion. I began with Karl Popper, the apostle of a "hard" demarcation between science and pseudo-science and realism, only to find an inner case for scepticism, historicism, and relativism. On the other hand, I join Michel Foucault, seen as a cultural relativist and modern sophist, with Popper's defense of objective knowledge. In matching their positions, I am suggesting that the debate on the historicity of reason and unreason is not a simple opposition between objectivist and subjectivist, or absolutist and relativist. If it were that simple the debate would not be worth discussing. I have followed the heuristic rule of suspicion; whenever a debate can be neatly classified, resist the temptation to analyze it that way.

The reason that philosophy cannot replicate strategies of success and progress is problem solving, or can only replicate them by being overtly sophistic, is because philosophical discussion concerns precisely the criteria for separating arguments, representations, and inquiries as reasonable/unreasonable or significant/irrelevant. The philosophical ways to defend such criteria or make such distinctions are always open to debate. I do not mean that therefore all positions are equally convincing. The point is that there is no intrinsic rightness about such distinctions or separations. Because there is no intrinsically correct strategy, strategies of reasoning are evaluated or defended in ways that themselves become objects of further philosophical dispute.

There are two typical responses to this dilemma about philosophical inquiry. First, some philosophical traditions hope that philosophical argument and its inherently undecidable debates can be dismissed as pseudo-arguments. What could be a better rhetorical strategy than demonstrating that your opponent's position is illusory? But, self-reflectively, the philosophical argument that all philosophical debate is illusory must itself be illusory. The second response separates philosophy as problem solving from philosophy as commentary. Philosophers should resolve disputes rather than reinterpret past attempts at resolution. In this spirit, Popper asks, what is the problem situation? The point is that only after the problem is clear can proposed answers be evaluated.

But why do problems arise? They are posed by traditions, even when they are taken from everyday life, science, the newspaper, or the philosopher's personal life. Precisely because these problems are not autonomous but embedded, the effort to resolve them or to evaluate solutions or, finally, to declare the question as meaningless, cannot be held apart – except by rhetorical technique – from historical commentary and reconstruction. Why philosophers today, for example, worry about mental states, but not "spiritual self-consciousness," or about natural kind terms, but not "substances," or about entailment, but not "self-evident ideas," is a problem of the historicity of inquiry and discourse. The quick reply is that these past concepts are really about our current questions, but in a poorly formulated, confused, or indirect manner. Then the strategy "we are clear, they were confused" is a defense in which one tradition is presented as universal, encompassing all others. But that strategy and its assumptions are not intrinsically true or exempt from debate, certainly, as I have argued, not simply because certain concepts are the familiar "paths" of current theorizing.

Can philosophy continue to talk in this reflective, self-questioning way? I have tried to understand arguments about historicism and consider the implications and criticisms of different positions. Why would I bother if all arguments are strategies and matters of tradition? Is not the historicist conclusion about debate and argument itself trapped within the prison-house of tradition? But the position I am discussing is not positivism. It does not say that philosophical disputes are meaningless. Historicism, therefore, does not require that argument, reasoning, and reflection be abandoned. It does require that appeals to such terms as self-evidence, common sense, demonstrative, pure, and a priori be reconstructed. These terms are not floating freely, available eternally for the construction of good reasoning. Reasoning is always local and locatable.

Philosophical reflection, short of some rhetorical defense, cannot be stopped short at some chosen standard, assumption, or primitive concept. Such criteria are relative to a style of inquiry. That argument does not denigrate the patient work of those who study and argue about mental states, entailment, or natural kind terms. Rather, it questions whether such inquiry is progressing in the solution to problems that are the same as the past dispute or in any more privileged position with regard to understanding the world than those past traditions, now confidently declared obsolete.

Historicism treats knowledge as a culturally significant system. It therefore treats philosophical reflection as an important aspect of that system, but not a privileged vantage point. As a kind of reflection, historicism makes statements about all traditions from the vantage point of some style of inquiry. It admits the role of assumptions and, therefore, does not claim that the world is transparent to its gaze. What is seen, understood, or taken as basic always depends on *when*. The various "shapes of knowledge," as Clifford Geertz calls them, are local, and thus philosophical reflection must resist a totalizing gesture. But historicism is not inconsistent, since it does not treat general statements as meaningless or illusory. Rather it treats generality and universality as provisional conclusions. The ability to separate out the transitory from the permanent, the core from the periphery or the constituted from the constitutive, is the result of lengthy, uncertain reconstructions of change in systems of knowledge. Historicism proposes that knowledge be studied as different ways in which the world is talked about, represented, cut up, ignored, suppressed, individuated, and generalized. None of these ways is about how the world is intrinsically; therefore, these arguments about the world are always oblique. The point is that the demonstration of how these arguments are commensurable, understandable, or solvable is always essentially contested. Certainty is a habit of interpretation, it is the intuitive inertia of the present.

The problems dealt with in this study concern "contested concepts," as W.B. Gallie calls them, namely inconclusive kinds of debates characteristic of interpretive disciplines. But the existence of these debates is not a scandal. The effort to show a universal condition for all disputes about the world is either practically futile or trivial. One can always argue, for instance, that what is being contested is just, for that very reason, not the universal and necessary condition for all thinking and theorizing.

Habermas, whose position I considered in the final chapter, argues that we need a standard of truth to distinguish between coerced and reasoned agreement. Habermas is making the historicist point that appeals to reason are contextual, and thus, upon analysis, may not have fully reflected or criticized the constraints in that context. Habermas's solution to this problem of reflection is a standard of truth as idealized consensus under conditions of unlimited communication and freedom from all domination maintained over time. Such a condition is not only idealized, as Habermas readily admits, but irrelevant to the debates I have considered. As a standard, it is futile and resolves no essentially contested concept; nor can it guide any historical reconstruction. Further, Habermas's view maintains the hermeneutic project of preventing misunderstanding or misreading; it assumes that historicity can be transcended.

To reconstruct the defense of objectivity is not to ignore the difference between reasoned and coerced agreement – though that difference is itself a problem of interpretation and a contested demonstration. But there is no hope of using that provisional distinction to discover which framework supplies the correct understanding of the world, preserves and maintains the correct reading against distortion and misunderstanding. Accepting the inevitability of misunderstanding, there is still a great deal to learn about how frameworks function and change. These studies would not be the story of knowledge – as though there is a hidden purpose behind all divergent schemes – but merely an account of how human schemes of representation can be fruitful, symbolic, useful, and even pure.

Does embracing such an approach lead, as many philosophers and educators recently have asserted, to intellectual and cultural ruin? Does it capitulate before diversity and uncertainty in standards, and suspicion about objectivity? Perhaps this often repeated lesson needs to be questioned, along with the implicit assumption that some kind of philosophical argument can suffice to impose a standard or truth *sub specie aeternitas*. Human history just as easily tells the story of how diversity, uncertainty, and tolerance benefited, as it does of how indeterminacy produced moral or theoretical weakness before the complex task of understanding. The prejudice or presuppositional framework which constitutes the world as the object of diverse manifestations cannot and does not attempt to prove the truth of those assumptions. It simply makes its case against the possibility of an innocent or neutral reading presented as a viable alternative to this indeterminacy.

Kant called the sceptic "a species of nomads, despising all settled modes of life." But Kant concluded that the sceptic is a "benefactor of human reason in so far as he compels us, . . . to keep watch, lest we consider as well-earned possession what we perhaps obtain only illegitimately." I have considered a way to "keep watch" over knowledge and "without sneers" treat this constant proliferation of systems of knowledge, so much a part of the modernist experience, as finally disruptive of those familiar and "settled modes of life."

Notes

Introduction

1. Donald Henahan, "Should We Care Who Wrote It?" Music View: Arts and Entertainment, *The New York Times* (July 12, 1987), p. 29.

2. In philosophy I have reviewed a debate parallel to the one in music over the study of Descartes's *Meditations*. See Robert D'Amico, "Text and Context: Derrida and Foucault on Descartes," in *The Structural Allegory*, ed. John Fekete (Minneapolis: University of Minnesota Press, 1984), pp. 164–82.

3. Martha Nussbaum, "Sophistry About Conventions" *New Literary History* Vol. 27, No. 1 (Autumn, 1985), pp. 129–39.

4. G. Iggers, *The German Conception of History* (Middleton: Wesleyan University Press, 1968).

5. Richard Burian, "More than a Marriage of Convenience: On the Inextricability of History and Philosophy of Science," *Philosophy of Science*, 44 (1977), p. 9.

1 Prophecy

1. Leo Alexander, "Medical Science Under Dictatorship" *The New England Journal of Medicine*, Vol. 241, no. 2 (July 14, 1949), pp. 39–47.

2. "After the publication of *The Open Society* in 1945 my wife pointed out to me that the book did not represent my central philosophical interests, for I was not primarily a political philosopher." Karl Popper, *The Unended Quest* (La Salle: Open Court, 1976), p. 148. But also in describing both *The Open Society* and *The Poverty of Historicism* Popper says "Both grew out of the theory of knowledge of *Logik der Forschung* and out of my conviction that our often unconscious views on the theory of knowledge . . . are decisive for out attitudes toward ourselves and towards politics" (*Unended Quest*, p. 115).

3. Karl Popper, *The Open Society and Its Enemies*, Vol. 2 (Princeton: Princeton University Press, 1971), p. 173.

4. Popper, *Open Society*, p. 170.

5. "[A]ll observation involves interpretation in the light of our theoretical knowledge, . . . pure observational knowledge, unadulterated by theory, would, if at all possible, be utterly barren and futile." Karl Popper, *Conjectures and Refutations* (New York: Harper and Row, 1968), p. 23.

6. Joan Robinson in *Economic Philosophy* (London: Penguin, 1964), p. 239f holds that the concept of value is not an "operational" concept but just a word. This empiricist criticism of the concept of value began with Bohm-Bawerk's analysis of Marx in which he rejects Marx's arguments about value because the concept does not come from experience and is "not in close touch with the facts. . . . Marx's system is not educed from the facts . . . by sound empiricism or a solid economico-psychological analysis." Eugen von Bohm-Bawerk, *Karl Marx and the Close of His System* (London: Merlin Press, 1975), p. 101. Also in M. Wolfson, *A Reappraisal of Marxian Economics* (New York: Columbia University Press, 1966) he concludes "we can observe prices . . . but we cannot observe value. Why not simply jettison the concept as a metaphysical philosopher's stone?" (p. 46).

7. David Ricardo, *Principles of Political Economy*, Vol. I, ed. Piero Sraffa and Maurice Dobb (Cambridge: Cambridge University Press, 1966), p. 14.

8. Popper, *Open Society*, p. 93.

9. Popper, *Open Society*, p. 175–76.

10. Popper states that he first defined his position on theory of knowledge as "methodological nominalism" because of his opposition to dogmatic essentialists like Plato. But he adds; "In the early 1920s I had two discussions. The first was a discussion with Karl Polanyi . . . [who] thought that what I described as 'methodological nominalism' was characteristic of the natural sciences but not of the social sciences. The second discussion . . . with Heinrich Gomperz . . . shocked me by describing my position as 'realist' in *both* sense of the word." *Unended Quest*, p. 20.

11. "Methodological rules are here regarded as *conventions*. They might be described as the rules of the game of empirical science. . . . The game of science is, in principle, without end. He who decides one day that scientific statements do not call for any further tests, and that they can be regarded as finally verified, retires from the game." Karl Popper, *Logic of Scientific Discovery* (New York: Harper Torchbooks, 1968), p. 53. In another context Popper says that he was always aware that theories could be "immunized" against falsification and suggests "there are, of course, also auxiliary hypotheses which are merely evasive immunizing moves. They decrease content. All this suggests the *methodological rule* not to put up with any content-decreasing manoeuvres." *Unended Quest*, p. 44. For an argument concerning the tension between Popper's fallibilist and realist positions seek Mark Amadeus Notturno, *Objectivity,*

Rationality and the Third Realm: Justification and the Grounds of Psychologism (Boston: Martinus Nijhoff, 1985), pp. 166–71.

12. Karl Marx, *Capital*, Vol. 1, trans. Ben Fowkes (London: Penguin, 1976), pp. 677–78.

13. Marx, *Capital*, p. 680.

14. John Weeks, *Capital and Exploitation* (London: Edward Arnold, 1981), pp. 36f.

15. Popper, *Open Society*, p. 8.

16. Popper, *Conjectures and Refutations*, p. 104.

17. Popper, *Conjectures and Refutations*, p. 105.

18. Marx did distinguish between appearance and essence. Popper defines essentialism as a position, which among other failings, denies the reality of appearances. Though Marx does define labor as the "essence" of a commodity he does not deny the reality of prices. Rather he concludes that prices are misleading as "facts." Marx is critical and suspicious of commonsense observation because of his theory of ideology. In a passage that seems to reply to Popper's position about supply and demand, Marx makes a realist argument.

> But he [the capitalist] tries to buy all commodities as cheaply as possible, and his own invariable explanation of his profit is that it is the result of mere sharp practice, of buying under the value and selling over it. Hence he never comes to see that if such a thing as the value of labor really existed, and he really paid this value, no capital would exist, and his money would never be transformed into capital. . . .
>
> For the rest, what is true of all appearance and their hidden background is also true of the form of appearance "value and price of labour" or "wages" as contrasted with the essential relation manifested in it, namely the value and price of labour power. The forms of appearance are reproduced, directly and spontaneously, as current and usual modes of thought; the essential relation must first be discovered by science. Classical political economy stumbles approximately onto the true state of affairs, but without consciously formulating it. It is unable to do this as long as it stays within its bourgeois skin.

Capital, Vol. i, p. 682.

19. Karl Popper, "Science: Conjectures and Refutations," in *Conjectures and Refutations*, pp. 33–65. There was no consistent political position among the positivists of the Vienna Circle but socialism was embraced by at least Otto Neurath in the essay "Empirical Sociology," which appears now in a collection of his writings entitled *Empiricism and Sociology*, ed. Marie Neurath and Robert S. Cohen (Boston: Reidel, 1973), pp. 319–420. In the same collection Neurath's essays on politics may have explicitly led Popper to his work on historicism. Neurath's "Utopia as a Social Engineer's Construction" asserts that "what yesterday was dreamers' work, today already appears as scientific work preparing the shaping of the future" (p. 151), and perhaps was a source

for Popper's section "Utopia and Piecemeal Engineering," in *The Poverty of Historicism* (Boston: Beacon Press, 1957), pp. 67–70. In the essay "Personal Life and Class Struggle" Neurath writes, in defense of Marxism, that:

> Marxism recognises science only where one can prophecy, that is derive one partial occurrence from another. But it is precisely scientific criticism that inhibits the Marxist from regarding long-range prophecies as possible. He knows how small is the number of historical conditions that we know, but he also applies to himself the Marxist doctrine of the dependence of our knowledge. . . . The Marxist, as a strict scientist, must admit that the course of history allows of various interpretations. (p. 293).

20. Popper, *Open Society*, p. 178.

21. Popper, *Conjectures and Refutations*, p. 37.

22. Marx, *Capital*, Vol. I, p. 531.

23. Popper, *Open Society*, p. 181.

24. "In Marx's day, nobody even thought of that technique of state intervention which is now called 'counter cycle policy' and, indeed, such a thought must be utterly foreign to an unrestrained capitalist system." Popper, *Open Society*, pp. 181–82.

25. Ingvar Johansson makes the argument that Popper does not apply his own methodological guidelines even to cases in the natural sciences. He asserts that in a complex debate with the physicist Niels Bohr over the so-called Copenhagen Interpretation of quantuam mechanics, against which Popper argued for some thirty years, Popper proposed an alternative theory which, Johansson claims, was clearly falsified.

> Popper proposes a theory having the consequences that the laws of conservation of energy and momentum are not true in the singular case, but experiments [in particle physics] show them to be true there, too. Popper's theory is falsified, but he has not rejected it! . . .
>
> Accordingly, my conclusion is simply that the quantum physicist Popper does not behave in accordance with the rules set up by Popper the philosopher of science. One of Popper's hypotheses is falsified and another ad hoc, but he has rejected neither of them.

Ingvar Johansson, *A critique of Karl Popper's methodology* (Oslo: Akameiforlaget, 1975), pp. 113–14.

26. Popper, *Open Society*, p. 197.

27. Imre Lakatos, "The Methodology of Research Programmes" in *Criticism and the Growth of Knowledge*, ed. Imre Lakatos and Alan Musgrave (London: Cambridge University Press, 1970), p. 116.

28. Hilary Putnam, "The 'Corroboration' of Theories," in *Mathematics, Matter and Method: Philosophical Papers*, Vol. I (New York: Cambridge University Press, 1975), p. 259.

29.   Popper, *Logic of Scientific Discovery*, p. 51. Popper continues: "The main problem of philosophy is the critical analysis of the appeal to the authority of 'experience' – precisely that 'experience' which every latest discoverer of positivism is, as ever, artlessly taking for granted. To such objections, however, the positivist only replies with a shrug: they mean nothing to him, since they do not belong to empirical science, which alone is meaningful. 'Experience' for him is a programme, not a problem." (pp. 51–52).

30.   Though I am not concerned here with a textual dispute about readings of Marx there is a great deal of evidence that Marx did not hold to a theory of inexorable stages of historical evolution. See W.A. Suchting, "Marx, Popper, and 'Historicism'," *Inquiry* Vol. 15, No. 3 (Autumn 1972), pp. 235–66; and Rober D'Amico, *Marx and Philosophy of Culture* (Gainesville: University of Florida Press, 1981).

31.   Popper, *Open Society*, p. 189. Popper's argument is that experience shows Marx to be wrong and that auxiliary hypotheses are simply trying to "explain away" experience. But Popper sometimes speaks of "criticism of experience" when he challenges dogmatic empiricism in the sciences. See footnote 29.

2   Situational Logic

1.   Certainly part of the confusion engendered by Popper's book was his idiosyncratic use of the term `historicism. In a review Herbert Marcuse comments in frustration: "In reading Popper's book, I often stopped and asked: against what is he really arguing? who has actually maintained what he is so efficiently destroying? And often I was unable to identify the attacked theory (especially since Popper is extremely sparing with references)." Marcuse, *Studies in Critical Philosophy* (Boston: Beacon Press, 1972), p. 197. The traditional conception of historicism is stated, for example, by Maurice Mandelbaum"

> This view of the world may express itself in many variant forms. Perhaps the most common is that which holds that every set of cultural values to be relative to the age in which it is dominant. This form of historicism, which we may best speak of as the historicity of values, is often identified with historicism as such. However, there is also a prevalent form of historicism which we may call that of knowledge. . . . historicism claims that no statement can be considered true or false without reference to the time at which it was formulated.

Mandelbaum, *The Problem of Historical Knowledge* (New York: Liveright Publishing, 1938), p. 89. Finally, Calvin Rand suggests that Popper's definition "goes as far as to contradict many genuine historicist principles and remains quite contrary to the spirit of even Vico's and Herder's historicist thinking." Rand, "Two Meanings of Historicism in the Writings of Dilthey, Troeltsche, and Meinecke," *Journal of the History of Ideas*, Vol. XXV, no. 4 (Oct.–Dec. 1964), p. 5165.

2. Karl Popper, *The Poverty of Historicism* (Boston: Beacon Press, 1957), pp. 3–4.

3. Karl Popper, *The Unended Quest* (La Salle: Open Court, 1976), p. 114.

4. "When we contrast the relative success of sociology with the success of physics, then we are assuming that success in sociology would likewise consist, basically, in the corroboration of predictions. It follows that certain methods – prediction with the help of laws, and the testing of laws by observation – must be common to physics and sociology. *I fully agree with this view* [emphasis added] in spite of the fact that I consider it one of the basic assumptions of historicism." Popper, *Poverty of Historicism*, pp. 35–36.

5. Rand, "Two Meanings of Historicism," pp. 507–8.

6. Karl Popper, *Objective Knowledge: An Evolutionary Approach* (Oxford: Clarendon Press, 1972), p. 162. Or this historicist passage: "And a good historian will add new fuel to this curiosity; he will make us wish to *understand* people, and situations, that we did not know about before." Popper, "A Pluralist Approach to Philosophy of History," in *Roads to Freedom*, ed. Erich Streissler (London: Routledge and Kegan Paul, 1969), p. 188.

7. Popper, *Poverty of Historicism*, p. 3.

8. Popper recounts the distinction made famous by Wilhelm Dilthey and still influential in philosophy; "Physics aims at casual explanation: sociology at an understanding of purpose or meaning." Popper, *Poverty of Historicism*, p. 20. In Popper's "A Pluralist Approach to Philosophy of History" he cites W. Windelband, H. Rickert, W. Dilthey and R.C. Collingwood, and in a footnote in *The Open Society and Its Enemies* Vol II (Princeton: Princeton University Press, 1966) he says: "Weber, following Rickert, repeatedly insists that our interest, in turn, depends upon idea of value; in this he is certainly not wrong. . . . None of these authors, however, draws the revolutionary consequence that since all history depends upon our interest, *there can only be histories and never a 'history,'* a story of the development of mankind 'as it happened'" (p. 364). Here Popper really seems to be concerned with what might be called "objectivism" – the identification of theory and reality. As Herbert Butterfield puts the point: "Therefore, we must beware even of saying, 'History says . . .' or 'History proves . . . ,' as though she herself were the oracle; as though indeed history, once she had spoken, had put the matter beyond the range of mere human inquiry." Butterfield, *The Whig Interpretation of History* (London: Bell and Sons, 1963), pp. 131–32.

9. Nicholas Tilley, "Popper, Historicism and Emergence," *Philosophy of the Social Sciences*, 12 (1982), pp. 59–67. In looking at Popper's reconstruction of a pro-historicist argument Tilley points out that it would be consistent, contrary to what Popper hopes to show, for the historicist to conclude: "There are no real laws, all generalizations may be confined to specific periods" (p. 60). Tilley's overall argument is that Popper adopted some

pro-historicist ideas, such as periodization, and that "the work on 'emergence' . . . contains, I shall suggest, a far more substantial anti-historicist message than the original *Poverty of Historicism*. But, paradoxically, this work also explains why historicist thinking is necessary whilst almost inevitably being mistaken" (p. 59). What generates Tilley's confusing position about Popper is that he accepts that Popper is an anti-historicist. My position is closer to James Farr, "Popper's Hermeneutics," *Philosophy of the Social Sciences*, 13 (1983), pp. 157–76.

10. Popper, *Poverty of Historicism*, p. 16.

11. "What Popper has to offer for history may be described as objectivity relative to a point of view. . . . in the sense . . . that everyone adopting the point of view will, in so far as he is rational and competent, tend to agree in his judgements of relevance, in his selections. . . . But there will be no objectivity in the full sense in the selection of points of view." R.F.Atkinson, *Knowledge and Explanation in History* (Ithaca: Cornel University Press, 1978), pp. 80–81.

12. Popper, "A Pluralist Approach to Philosophy of History," p. 197.

13. Popper, *Open Society*, p. 267.

14. Popper, *Poverty of Historicism*, p. 151.

15. "I owe the suggestion that it was Marx who first conceived social theory as the study of unwanted social repercussions of nearly all our actions to K. Polanyi." Popper, *Open Society*, p. 323, f. 11.

16. Popper, *Open Society*, p. 176.

17. "For Popper, we can never at any level get out of our theoretical structures to attain reality itself. All we have are successions of frameworks. Theory-less reality is a myth. . . . Certainly it would give us no licence to argue in favour of an optimistic realism about science, itself perhaps the product of an uncritical acceptance of certain scientific ways of speaking and thinking." Anthony O'Hear, *Karl Popper* (London: Routledge and Kegan Paul, 1980), pp. 206–7. O'Hear mentions earlier that, "it is as if he [Popper] wants to soften the effects of his scepticism, and it is undeniable that, without some such softening, few would follow him far" (p. 206).

18. Karl Popper, *Conjectures and Refutations* (London: Routledge and Kegan Paul, 1963), p. 104.

19. Popper, *Conjectures and Refutations*, p. 105.

20. Popper, *Open Society*, pp. 268–69.

21. Popper, *Poverty of Historicism*, p. 137

22. Popper, *Poverty of Historicism*, p. 139

23. Popper, *Poverty of Historicism*, pp. 140–41.

24. Popper, *Poverty of Historicism*, p. 145.

25. Popper, *Poverty of Historicism*, p. 146.

26. Popper, "A Pluralist Approach to Philosophy of History," p. 196.

27. Popper, *Open Society*, p. 266.

28. Popper, *Objective Knowledge*, p. 179

29. Popper, *Open Society*, p. 374.

30. Hilary Putnam *Realism and Reason: Philosophical Papers*, Vol. 3 (London: Cambridge University Press, 1983), p. 188.

3 Conceptual Schemes

1. P.F. Strawson, *Individuals: An Essay in Descriptive Metaphysics* (London: Methuen, 1959) and *The Bounds of Sense* (London:Methuen, 1966). In *The Bounds of Sense*, which is Strawson's study of Kant, he begins with the statement: "It is possible to imagine kinds of world very different from the world as we know it. It is possible to describe types of experience very different from the experience we actually have" (p. 15). Strawson then introduces the Kantian theme that "there are limits to what we can conceive of, or make intelligible to ourselves, as a possible general structure of experience" (p. 15). But later Strawson suggests that the Kantian program of finding fundamental structures of any intelligible experience was a failure.

> [W]hat other [programme] are we prepared to offer? To this I can only reply that I see no reason why any high doctrine at all should be necessary here. The set of ideas, or schemes of thought, employed by human beings reflect, of course, their nature, their needs and their situation. . . . But it is no matter for wonder if conceivable variations are intelligible. . . . There is nothing here to demand, or permit, an explanation such as Kant's. (p. 44).

2. Rudolf Carnap, "Empiricism, Semantics, and Ontology," in *Meaning and Necessity* (Chicago: University of Chicago Press, 1956).

3. Carnap, "Empiricism," p. 207.

4. Carnap, "Empiricism," p. 208.

5. James Conant, *Science and Common Sense* (New Haven: Yale University Press, 1951).

6. Conant, *Science and Common Sense*, p. 25.

7. Conant, *Science and Common Sense*, p. 28.

8. Conant, *Science and Common Sense*, p. 36.

9. Hilary Putnam, *Realism and Reason"* *Philosophical Papers*, Vol. 3 (New York: Cambridge University Press, 1983), p. 230.

10. Conant, *Science and Common Sense*, pp 181–82.

11. Conant, *Science and Common Sense*, pp. 262–63.

12. Thomas Kuhn, *The Copernican Revolution* (New York: Vintage Books, 1959), p. 39.

13. Kuhn, *Copernican Revolution*, pp. 76–77.

14. W.V.O. Quine, "Two Dogmas of Empiricism," in *From a Logical Point of View* (New York: Harper Torchbooks, 1961).

15. Quine, "Two Dogmas," p. 42.

16. Conant, *Science and Common Sense*, pp. 44–45.

17. Paul Feyerabend, *Against Method* (London: New Left Books, 1975).

18. Ian Hacking, "Language, Truth and Reason," in *Rationality and Relativism*, ed. Martin Hollis and Steven Lukes (Oxford: Basil Blackwell, 1982), pp. 64–65.

19. "Accordingly, then, the writing-down effects a transformation of the original mode of being of the meaning. . . . It becomes sedimented, so to speak." Edmund Husserl, "The Origin of Geometry" in *Crisis of the European Sciences* (Evanston: Northwestern University Press, 1970), p. 361. See also Robert D'Amico, "Husserl on the Foundational Structures of Natural and Cultural Sciences," *Philosophy and Phenomenological Research*, Vol. XLII, no. 1 (September 1981), pp. 5–22.

20. Feyerabend, *Against Method*, p. 91.

21. In a recent reassessment of Galileo's relationship to theology Stillman Drake (perhaps with Feyerabend in mind) writes:
> [T]here is a widespread belief that Galileo, without adequate scientific evidence, battled from his earliest years for the Copernican system. . . . The common assumption that Galileo was a Copernican zealot has resulted in sharply conflicting pictures of his . . . personality. . . . In one picture, Galileo was an intuitive hero of science who, without sufficient evidence, did battle against benighted tradition; in another, he was an irresponsible trouble-maker . . . I believe both should be [discarded].

Drake, *Galileo* (New York: Hill and Wang, 1980), pp. 2–3.

22. "The 'internal/external' distinction presupposes that there is some central core of theory and sets of extraneous factors may or may not be pertinent to the treatment of certain questions concerning this hard core. I can see no justification for such a presupposition. . . . Which questions we want answers to will determine how we characterise discourses and what factors we include in this characterisation." Stephen Gaukroger, *Explanatory Structures* (New Jersey: Humanities Press, 1978), pp. 12–13.

23. For the argument connecting conceptual schemes to idealism see Jay Rosenberg, *One World and Our Knowledge of It: The Problematic of Realism in Post-Kantian Perspective* (Boston: Reidel, 1980); and Donald Davidson, "On the Very Notion of a Conceptual Scheme," *Inquiries into Truth and Interpretation* (New York: Oxford University Press, 1984).

24. Pierre Duhem, *The Aim and Structure of Physical Theory* (Princeton: Princeton University Press, 1954).

25. Duhem, *Aim and Structure of Physical Theory*, p. 159.

26. Duhem, *Aim and Structure of Physical Theory*, p. 152.

27. "How one employs accepted theories to explain familiar phenomena falling under them has not been the issue; rather we have tried to explore the geography of some dimly-lit passages along which the physicists have moved from surprising, anomalous data to a theory which might explain those data. We have discussed the obstacles which litter those passages. They are rarely of a direct observational or experimental variety, but always reveal conceptual elements. The observations and the experiments are infused with the concepts; they are loaded with the theories. When the natural philosopher is faced with the types of problem which we have been describing, his observations and his experiments will contain that problem. Galileo's geometrical bias, Kepler's perfect circle, Priestly's phlogiston, Leverrier's unobserved masses – these were the obstacles, *so we say now with the wisdom of hindsight*, [emphasis added]." R.N. Hanson, *Patterns of Discovery* (New York: Cambridge University Press, 1969), pp. 157–58.

28. Kuhn, *The Structure of Scientific Revolutions* (Chicago: University of Chicago Press, 1962), pp. 55–56.

29. J.B. Conant, ed., *Harvard Case Histories in Experimental Science*: "Overthrow of the Phlogiston Theory," Vol. 1 (Cambridge: Harvard University Press, 1957), pp. 72–73.

30. Alan Musgrave, "Why did oxygen supplant phlogiston?" *Method and Appraisal in the Physical Sciences: The Critical Background to Modern Science, 1800–1905*, ed. Colin Howson (New York: Cambridge University Press, 1976), pp. 189f.

31. Kenneth S. Davis, *The Cautionary Scientists: Priestly, Lavoisier, and the Founding of Modern Chemistry* (New York: Putnam's Sons, 1966), pp. 145f.

32. Conant, ed., "Overthrow of the Phlogiston Theory," p. 84.

33. Conant, ed., "Overthrow of the Phlogiston Theory," p. 84. Henry Guerlac argues: "It could hardly have been Priestly, or any other British chemist, whom Lavoisier was to conjure up as a rival when, to assure himself priority, he set down his brilliant discoveries . . . of 1772. . . . Yet this is what Lavoisier wanted posterity to believe. Years later, when preparing this famous note for publication, he altered – without regard to the Muse of History – the words of its final paragraph." Guerlac, *Lavoisier – The Crucial Year* (Ithaca: Cornell University Press, 1961), p. 75.

34. Louis Althusser, *Reading Capital* (New York: Pantheon, 1970), p. 146.

35. Frederick Engels, "Preface," *Capital*, Vol. 2 (New York: International Publishers, 1972), p. 14.

36. Engels, "Preface," p. 15.

37. Engels, "Preface," p. 15.

4 Rational Reconstruction

1. W.V.O. Quine, "Two Dogmas of Empiricism," in *From a Logical Point of View* (New York: Harper Torchbooks, 1961) pp. 42f.

2. "History of science, of course, is full of accounts of how crucial experiments allegedly killed theories. But these accounts are fabricated long after the theory had been abandoned." Imre Lakatos, *The Methodology of Scientific Research Programmes: Philosophical Papers*, Vol. I, ed. John Worral and Gregory Currie (New York: Cambridge University Press, 1978), p. 4. "Popper's great negative crucial experiments *disappear*; 'crucial experiment' is an honorific title, which may of course, be conferred on certain anomalies, but only *long after the event*, only when one programme has been defeated by another one" (p. 111).

3. Lakatos, *Methodology of Scientific Research*, p. 117.

4. Imre Lakatos, *Mathematics, Science and Epistemology: Philosophical Papers*, Vol. 2, ed. John Worral and Gregory Currie (New York: Cambridge University Press, 1978), p. 221.

5. Imre Lakatos, "Why did Copernicus' Research Programme Supersede Ptolemy's?", *Methodology of Scientific Research*, pp. 168–92. *Methodology of Scientific Research* is hereafter cited in the text by page numbers.

6. Lakatos claims "But Ptolemy's system (any given version of it) was commonly known to be refuted and anomaly-ridden long before Copernicus," *Methodology of Scientific Research*, p. 171. But as with many of his historical reconstructions he does not give any documentary evidence.

7. In a recent work Husain Sarkar presents Lakatos as proposing a way to choose between competing methods. "Lakatos claims correctly that in order to evaluate a scientific theory one has to move up to the level of method; to evaluate a method one has to move a step higher onto the level of meta-method. . . . We need not, however, move any higher; after all, says Lakatos, we need to stop somewhere so we may as well use the plane of meta-method as the agreed-upon stopping point." Sarkar, *A Theory of Method* (Berkeley: University of California Press, 1983), p. 51. Though Sarkar's book is filled with historical examples he claims to be arguing against the view that history of science should arbitrate between methodologies. Sarkar grants that studies of methodology have been dominated by a historiographical model of retrospective rationality. "Most, if not all philosophers of science agree . . . : a method should be judged in the light of the history of science. Failure to conform to the rational episodes in the history of science is considered a serious inadequacy in a method . . . I shall dub it . . . the *backward-looking* view. To show that this view is erroneous and too narrow for solving other methodological problems is my most important and central aim" (p. 5). Thus Sarkar tries to salvage Lakatos by separating his approach from retrospective historicism – the view I am drawing out of Lakatos – and stressing prescriptivism: "Methodological statements, like

statements in ethics, should be regarded as normative statements, possessors of truth-value" (p. x).

8. Paul Feyerabend, *Against Method* (London: New Left Books, 1975), p. 17.

9. Lakatos, "Understanding Toulmin," *Mathematics, Science and Epistemology*, pp. 224–43.

10. Lakatos, *Mathematics, Science and Epistemology*, pp. 237–38.

11. Lakatos, *Mathematics, Science and Epistemology*, p. 226.

12. "One may rationally stick to a degenerating programme until it is overtaken by a rival *and even after*. What one must *not* do is to deny its poor public record. Both Feyerbend and Kuhn conflate *methodological* appraisal of a programme with firm *heuristic* advice about what to do. It is perfectly rational to play a risky game: what is irrational is to deceive oneself about the risk." *Methodology of Scientific Research*, p. 117. Here, as in many passages, Lakatos shifts to a prescriptive ideal of rationality which by definition is immune from historical counterexamples. For this reason critics like Husain Sarkar recommend that Lakatos abandon appeals to the history of science entirely.

13. Noretta Koertge, summarizes;

> I have argued that Lakatos's challenge to externalists or *descriptivists* . . . is unfair because the historical data base which is to decide between them is deliberately rigged so as only to include "rational" episodes. . . . Lakatos has made the *a priori* assumption that the best examples of present (and past) scientific method cannot be improved upon. Therefore he rejects *out of hand* any theory of rationality which would reform orthodox scientific practices.

N. Koertge, "Rational Reconstructions," in *Essays in Memory of Imre Lakatos*, eds. R.S. Cohen, P.K. Feyerabend and M.W. Wartofsky (Boston: Reidel, 1976), p. 366.

14. "At one stage in the development of Imre's philosophy of science, he was clearly tempted by the notion that these standards might be timeless and a-historical. . . . Yet by 1973 . . . he . . . abandoned this notion. Still my own [view] . . . apparently roused Imre Lakatos to wrath. He used to denounce this view as intolerable elitist. . . . In the course of these exchanges I was never able . . . to fathom just what was leading Imre to such extremes; and I was particularly perplexed, when I recalled how far my own views about the judgment of conceptual change in natural science had been strengthened by reading . . . *Proofs and Refutations*. . . . I could only conclude that his rejection of anything associated with Ludwig Wittgenstein had been picked up by contagion, through his close association with Karl Popper, and so was scarcely more than an historical curiosity – a late, irrelevant echo of Old Vienna." Stephen Toulmin, "History, Praxis and the 'Third World'," in Cohen, Feyerabend, and Wartofsky, eds., *Essays in Memory of Imre Lakatos*, p. 656.

15. Ian Hacking, *Representing and Intervening* (New York: Cambridge University Press, 1984), p. 126.

16. Hacking, *Representing*, pp. 257, 260.

17. Hacking, *Representing*, p. 125.

18. Hacking, *Representing*, pp. 260–61.

19. Feyerabend, *Against Method*, pp. 196–97.

20. Hacking, *Representing*, p. 16.

5 Historical A Priori

1. Hilary Putnam, *Reason, Truth and History* (New York: Cambridge University Press, 1981), pp. 159–60.

2. Putnam, *Reason, Truth and History*, p. 156.

3. The best overview of Foucault's work can be found in Hubert L. Dreyfus and Paul Rabinow, *Michel Foucault: Beyond Structuralism and Hermeneutics* (Chicago: University of Chicago Press, 1982).

4. Michel Foucault, *The Order of Things* (New York: Pantheon, 1971), p. 127.

5. Michel Foucault, *The Birth of the Clinic: An Archaeology of Medical Perception*, trans. A.M. Sheridan Smith (New York: Pantheon, 1973), p. 3. Hereafter cited in the text by page numbers.

6. Lester J. King, *Medical Thinking: A Historical Preface* (Princeton: Princeton University Press, 1982):

> The scientific revolution . . . dampened scientific interest in imma-terial entities and directed attention to what could be observed, weighed, and measured. Such concepts as soul, archeus, and immaterial substance were extruded from science and shunted over to religion or to mysticism. In the resulting intellectual climate the nominalist position could prevail: immaterial entities like substantial forms were not real but merely verbal entities, *flatus vocis* abstracted from something truly real. . . . A new ontology with a materialistic base began to emerge. The entity behind the disease symptoms was asserted to be something material, something observable and measurable." (pp. 179–80).

King shows how the new ontology of disease as the result of a causal, material entity was a theoretical construction. Causes require conceptual entities embedded in theories.

> When we try to give causes of causes, we soon leave behind anything that we can see and feel and fall back on abstractions, on conceptual entities like a disproportion and coction, for the Greeks, or, for present day medicine, on cholesterol metabolism and the complexities of liver function. In ancient and modern medicine alike we would be leaving the realm of the concrete to rely on the abstract.

Abstractions (or relationships) we cannot see. They are conceptual entities, the products of reason, requiring mental activity for their creation and mental activity for their appreciation. (p. 193).

7. Larry Laudan, *Progress and Its Problems: Towards a Theory of Scientific Growth* (Berkeley: University of California Press, 1977), p. 177.

8. Foucault, *The Order of Things*, p. 127. Hereafter cited in the text by page numbering.

9. Laudan, *Progress*, pp. 180–81.

10. Laudan argues, echoing Foucault, that "specific cannons of rationality are time dependent." *Progress*, p. 187. He also makes history indispensable to the appraisal of theories "no sensible rational appraisal can be made of any doctrine without a rich knowledge of its historical development (and of the history of its rivals)" (p. 193). Hereafter cited in the text by page numbers.

11. Foucault admits that at the level of propositions the concept of truth is "neither arbitrary, nor modifiable, nor institutional," but he believes that truth at the level of discourse or theoretical system is "historical, modifiable, institutionally constraining." These views are discussed in Foucault's 1970 inaugural lecture, *L'ordre du discours*, where he argues: "But this will to truth, like the other system of exclusion, relies on institutional support: it is both reinforced and accompanied by whole strata of practices such as pedagogy . . . But it is probably even more profoundly accompanied by the manner in which knowledge is employed in a society, the way in which it is exploited, divided and, in some ways, attributed." Foucault, *Archaeology of Knowledge*, trans. A.M. Sheridan Smith (New York: Pantheon, 1972), p. 219. Nelson Goodman has taken a similar stand:

> Truth, far from being a solemn and severe master is a docile and obedient servant. The scientists who supposes that he is single-mindedly dedicated to the search for the truth deceives himself. . . . He as much decrees as discovers the laws he sets forth, as much designs as discerns the patterns he delineates. . . .
>
> Rather than speak of pictures as true or false we might better speak of theories as right or wrong; for the truth of the laws of a theory is but one special feature and is often, as we have seen, overridden in importance by the cogency and compactness and comprehensiveness, the informativeness and organizing power of the whole system.

Goodman, *Ways of Worldmaking* (Indianapolis: Hackettt, 1978), pp. 18–19.

12. Larry Laudan attacks Foucault, in a short footnote, for his obscure scepticism. "To understand a classic text, for Foucault, is neither to relate it to the biography of its author nor to examine the arguments within; rather the historian studies such texts in order to find out what they tell us about the (linguistic) consciousness of an era. . . . Foucaultian structuralism must rank as one of the most obscurantist historiographical fashions of the twentieth

century." *Progress*, p. 241. Of course, in my understanding of Foucault he does *not* study the consciousness of a period or its linguistic structures.

13. Foucault, *The Order of Things*, pp. 157–58. Hereafter cited in the text by page numbers.

14. Foucault, *The Archaeology of Knowledge*, p. 130.

6   Objective Knowledge

1. Plato, *The Collected Dialogues* ed. Edith Hamilton and Huntington Cairns (New York: Pantheon, 1961); *The Statesman*, p. 1055 (287c).

p. 121.   *'ected Dialogues; Phaedrus*, p. 511 (265e).

3. Imre Lakatos argues that prior to Newton, seventeenth century thought began to doubt ultimate answers and encouraged a skeptical and tolerant enlightenment. In lieu of an ultimate truth the standard for selecting hypotheses was simplicity, precisely because of debate in astronomy in which the hypothesis that could simply "save the phenomena" was accepted. Lakatos, "Newton's Effect on Scientific Standards," *The Methodology of Scientific Research Programmes: Philosophical Papers*, Vol. 1 ed. John Worral and Gregory Currie (New York: Cambridge University Press, 1978), pp. 199f; and Pierre Duhem, *Saving the Phenomena* trans. Edmund Dolan and Chaninah Maschler (Chicago: University of Chicago Press, 1985), Chap. 7.

4. Foucault's translator, A.M. Sheridan Smith, renders Foucault's extensive use of the term *les enonces* (and such variants as *la fonction enonciative* or *la configuration du champ enonciatif*) with the term "statements." Though the direct choice of "enunciation" is misleading because it suggests a spoken expression, "statement" is somewhat confusing because of its different use in Anglo-American philosophy. Perhaps the term "inscription" captures the objectivity of discourse that Foucault seeks to convey when he says:

> The repeatable materiality that characterizes the enunciative [inscriptive] function reveals the statement [inscription] as a specific and paradoxical object, but also as one of those objects that men produce, manipulate, use, transform, exchange, combine, decompose and recompose, and possibly destroy. . . . Thus the statement [inscription] circulates, is used, disappears, allows or prevents the realization of a desire, serves or resists various interests, participates in challenge and struggle, and becomes a theme of appropriation or rivalry.

Foucualt, *Archaeology of Knowledge* trans. A.M. Sheridan Smith (New York: Pantheon, 1972), p. 105. To avoid further confusion I will simply follow Sheridan Smith's translation in the following discussion. *Archaeology of Knowledge* is hereafter cited in the text by page number.

5. "Presumably, . . . each [speech] act is embodied in a statement and each statement contains one of those acts. . . . Yet such a correlation does not stand up to examination." Foucault, *Archaeology*, p. 83.

6. "I showed earlier that it was neither by 'words' nor by 'things' that the regulation of the objects proper to a discursive formation should be defined; similarly, it must now be recognized that it is neither by recourse to a transcendental subject nor by recourse to a psychological subjectivity that the regulation of its enunciations should be defined." Foucault, *Archaeology*, p. 55. I will discuss the transcendental approach in my conclusion, but for an account of what he calls a "neo-transcendental" argument, different from Kant's, see Gerd Buchdahl, "Neo-Transcendental Approaches Towards Scientific Theory Appraisal," in *Science, Belief and Behaviour*, ed. D.H. Mellor (Cambridge, Cambridge University Press, 1980), pp. 1–21.

7. Martin Heidegger, "The Age of the World View," in *The Question of Technology and Other Essays*, trans. William Lovitt (New York: Harper and Row, 1977), p. 121

8. Stephen Gaukroger makes a Foucaultian point about the study of theoretical discourse.

> First theoretical discourses are not differentiated "in nature." They can only be differentiated on the basis of some theoretical classification. . . . Secondly, theoretical discourses cannot be differentiated as such, they can only be differentiated in virtue of their having distinct epistemological structures. . . . Thirdly, different characterisations of discourses may include very different factors, depending on the questions that we want answers to.

Stephen Gaukroger, *Explanatory Structures* (New Jersey: Humanities Press, 1978), pp. 11–12.

9. Michel Foucault, "La Poussiere et le Nuage," in *L'Impossible Prison* (Paris: Editions du Seuil, 1980), pp. 34–35.

10. Michel Foucault, "What is an Author?," *Language, Counter-Memory, Practice*, ed. Donald Bouchard (Ithaca: Cornell University Press, 1977).

11. This issue is not the only point at which the thought of Foucault and Popper converge, as can be seen in the following quote from Foucault:

> History has no "meaning," though this is not to say that it is absurd or incoherent. On the contrary, it is intelligible and should be susceptible of analysis down to the smallest detail – but this in accordance with the intelligibility of struggle, of strategies and tactics. Neither the dialectic, as logic of contradiction, nor semiotics, as the structure of communication, can account for the intrinsic intelligibility of conflicts. "Dialectic" is a way of evading the always open and hazardous reality of conflict by reducing it to a Hegelian skeleton, and "semiology" is a way of avoiding its violent, bloody and lethal character by reducing it to the calm Platonic form of language and dialogue.

Foucault, *Power/Knowledge* ed. Colin Gordon (New York: Pantheon, 1980), pp. 114–15.

12. Karl Popper's discussion of the third domain occurs primarily in "Epistemology Without a Knowing Subject" and "On the Theory of the Objective Mind," in Popper, *Objective Knowledge: An Evolutionary Epistemology* (Oxford: Clarendon Press, 1972). Some helpful commentaries in the critical literature on Popper are: James Farr, "Popper's Hermeneutics" *Philosophy of the Social Sciences*, 13 (1983), pp. 157–76; Gregory Currie, "Popper's Evolutionary Epistemology: A Critique," *Synthese*, 37 (1978), pp. 413–31; John Krige, "A Critique of Popper's Conception of the Relationship Between Logic, Psychology, and a Critical Epistemology," *Inquiry*, Vol. 21, no. 3 (Autumn, 1978), pp. 313–35; Peter Skagestad, *Making Sense of History* (Oslo: Universitesforlaget, 1975); Mark Amadeus Notturno, *Objectivity, Rationality and the Third Realm: Justification and the Grounds of Psychologism* (Boston: Martinus Nijhoff, 1985).

13. Popper, *Objective Knowledge*, pp. 160–61.

14. Popper, *Objective Knowledge*, p. 109. In *The Open Society*, Popper offers a surprising argument about the need for presuppositions: "That is to say, a rationalist attitude must be first adopted if any argument or experience is to be effective, and it cannot therefore be based upon argument or experience. . . . But we are also free to choose a critical form of rationalism, one which frankly admits its origin in an irrational decision (and which, to that extent, admits a certain priority of irrationalism)." *The Open Society and Its Enemies*, Vol. 2 (Princeton: Princeton University Press, 1971), pp. 230–31. In the addenda to this volume Popper glossed this statement with his argument that every example of fallibilism produces an *advance of knowledge* based on learning from errors and criticizing mistakes. Thus situational analysis will show that "science is fallible because science is human" but not capitulate to scepticism about knowledge.

15. Popper, *Objective Knowledge*, p. 155, 159.

16. Popperians have sometimes worried that their criteria may turn out to be psychological. In discussing Popper's phrase "severity of tests," as an interpretation of degree of corroboration, Alan Musgrave admits: "These passages seem to make the severity of a test depend in part upon the psyche of the tester. For the *sincerity* with which a test is devised and performed seems to be distinctively psychological, to depend upon the state of mind of him who performs it." Musgrave then suggests: "The intuitive idea behind this objective analysis is that the more unlikely or unexpected (in light of what we already know, of our 'background knowledge') is a prediction . . . then the more severe will be the test . . ." Musgrave, "Objectivism of Popper's Epistemology," in *The Philosophy of Karl Popper*, ed. Paul Arthur Schilpp (La Salle: Open Court, 1974), p. 577. It is hard to see, however, how "unexpected or unllikely" eliminate the psychologistic implication of "sincerity." Notturno, in *Objectivity, Rationality and the Third Realm*, p. 161, argues that the only way to meet this objection is to stress that Popper does not entirely eliminate beliefs. He allows them but only for the purpose of generating criticism and not as justification, either by sincerity or strength.

17. Nelson Goodman, *Languags of Art* (Indianapolis: Hackett, 1976), Chap. 3.

18. See Walter Benjamin, "The Work of Art in the Age of Mechanical Reproduction," in *Illuminations*, ed. Hannah Arendt (New York: Shocken, 1969)."

19. Popper, *Objective Knowledge*, p. 254. In his "Replies to My Critics" Popper adds that: "Institutions are, I believe, man-made, and we are therefore greatly responsible for them. But they have a certain degree of autonomy: they belong to world 3. And just as mathematics is not wholly arbitrary (though different systems of mathematics are possible . . .) so it is with social institutions. And if science is a social institution, so is its autonomous aim, the search for objective truth. . . . I am not a conventionalist . . . but a defender of the autonomy of the objective world 3, in which objective truth plays a major role." Popper, *The Philosophy of Karl Popper*, p. 1116.

20. Nelson Goodman, *Ways of Worldmaking* (Indiannapolis: Hackett, 1978). In this book Goodman adopts what he calls a "non-Kantian theme" about the "multiplicity of worlds." Goodman is led to historicist views about science and art. "Ironically then, our passion for *one* world is satisfied, at different times and for different purposes, in *many* different ways. Not only motion derivation, weighing, order, but even reality is relative." Goodman, *Ways of Worldmaking*, p. 20. In relation to aesthetics he argues: "An object may symbolize different things at different times, and nothing at other times. An inert or purely utilitarian object may come to function as art, and a work of art may come to function as an inert or purely utilitarian object. Perhaps, rather than art being long and life short, both are transient." Goodman, *Ways of Worldmaking*, p. 70.

21. Popper, *Objective Knowledge*, p. 115–16.

22. "A satisfactory understanding will be reached if the interpretation, the conjectural theory, finds support in the fact that it can throw new light on new problems – on more problems than we expected; or if it finds support in the fact that it explains may sub-problems, some of which were not seen to start with." Popper, *Objective Knowledge*, pp. 164–65.

23. Popper, *Objective Knowledge*, p. 174.

24. Popper, *Objective Knowledge*, p. 185.

25. Goodman, *The Ways of Worldmaking*, p. 18.

26. Popper, *Objective Knowledge*, p. 189.

7   Transcendental Turn

1. Michel Foucault, *The Birth of the Clinic*, trans. A.M. Sheridan Smith (New York: Pantheon Books, 1973), p. 65. There is a good introductory discussion to this problem in David Papineau's *For Science in the Social Sciences* (New York: St. Martin's Press, 1978). In his chapter "Alien Belief Systems," Papineau asks "How is it possible to find out what alien people think in the first place? This is a deceptively deep question and needs to be answered with care" (p. 134).

2. Jay Rosenberg, *One World and Our Knowledge of It: The Problematic of Realism in Post-Kantian Perspective* (Boston: Reidel, 1980), p. 88. Rosenberg concludes that the problem of a world "ineffable and incognizable" is simply part of "these great and classical puzzles . . . icons of the Myth of the Mind Apart" (p. 191).

3. Rosenberg, *One World and Our Knowledge of It*, p. 107.

4. Claude Levi-Strauss, *The Savage Mind* (Chicago: University of Chicago Press, 1966), p. 6.

5. Levi-Strauss, *The Savage Mind*, p. 3.

6. Levi-Strauss, *The Savage Mind*, p. 9.

7. Robin Horton, "African Traditional Thought and Western Science: Part I. From Tradition to Science; Part II. The 'Closed' and the 'Open' Predicament," *Africa* 37 (1967), pp. 52–71, 155–187.

8. E.E. Evans-Pritchard, *Witchcraft, Oracles and Magic Among the Azande* (Oxford: Clarendon Press, 1976). "It will have been noted that the Azande act experimentally within the framework of their mystical notions. . . . Each seance must be in itself experimentally consistent . . . they reason excellently in the idiom of their beliefs, but they cannot reason outside, or against, their beliefs because they have no other idiom in which to express their thoughts" (pp. 158–59). Evans-Pritchard also specifies, again in conformity with our thought experiment about conceptual schemes, that doubts actually reinforce the practice. "Azande are only sceptical of particular oracles and not of oracles in general, and their scepticism is always expressed in a mystical idiom that vouches for the validity of the poison oracle as an institution" (p. 163).

9. Donald Davidson, *Inquiries into Truth and Interpretation* (New York: Oxford University Press, 1984).

10. Dan Sperber, *Rethinking Symbolism* (New York: Cambridge University Press, 1975), pp. 3–4.

11. Davidson, *Inquiries into Truth*, pp. 196–97.

12. Davidson, *Inquiries into Truth*, p. 195.

13. Davidson, *Inquiries into Truth*, p. 198.

14. A.C. Grayling, *The Refutation of Scepticism* (La Salle: Open Court Publishing, 1985), Chap. 3.

15. Kant, *Critique of Practical Reason*, trans. Lewis White Beck (New York: Bobbs-Merrill, 1956), pp. 54–55.

16. P.F. Strawson, *The Bounds of Sense* (London: Methuen, 1966), p. 15. In Barry Stroud's *The Significance of Philosophical Scepticism* (Oxford: Clarendon Press, 1984), Chap. 4 he argues that transcendental arguments are really verificationist because they "deflate" scepticism by declaring it meaningless. If Stroud is correct, then the notorious problems with the verification theory of meaning would raise serious doubts about arguing for necessary presuppositions of experience. I agree with Stroud's treatment of transcendental

arguments, but in the following discussion I still assume that they are distinct from the verificationist theory of meaning.

17.   Grayling, *Refutation of Scepticism*, p. 83.

18.   Grayling, *Refutation of Scepticism*, pp. 92–93.

19.   Jürgen Habermas, "A Postscript to *Knowledge and Human Interests*," *Philosophy of the Social Sciences*, 3 (1973), p. 171.

20.   Grayling, *Refutation of Scepticism*, p. 109.

21.   Jürgen Habermas, *Knowledge and Human Interests*, trans. Jeremy J. Shapiro (Boston: Beacon Press, 1971), p. 12.

22.   Habermas, *Knowledge and Human Interests*, pp. 35–36.

23.   Habermas, *Knowledge and Human Interests*, p. 195.

24.   Jürgen Habermas, *Toward a Rational Society*, trans. Jeremy J. Shapiro (Boston: Beacon Press, 1970), p. 84. Habermas is attacking the anti-instrumentalist philosophy of science that Herbert Marcuse presents in *One-Dimensional Man* (Boston: Beacon Press, 1967). Marcuse argues that making concepts synonymous with sets of operations or technical control is anti-critical and anti-historical. He says, "operational rationality is a *suppression* of history" p. 97.

25.   Habermas, *Toward a Rational Society*, p. 88.

26.   Habermas, "A Postscript to *Knowledge and Human Interests*," p. 169.

27.   Habermas, "A Postscript to *Knowledge and Human Interests*, p. 171.

28.   Jürgen Habermas, "What is Universal Pragmatics?" in *Communication and the Evolution of Society*, trans. Thomas McCarthy (Boston: Beacon Press, 1979), p. 21.

29.   Habermas, *The Theory of Communicative Action*, trans. Thomas McCarthy (Boston: Beacon Press, 1981).

30.   Habermas, "What is Universal Pragmatics?," p. 24.

Index

a posteriori 143
a priori 90, 132, 140, 143, 146
abstraction 162, 163
ad hoc 66
aesthetics ix, 167
Alexander, L. 1, 2, 150
allographic 110
Althusser, L. 49, 159
analytic 37
anomally 60
anthropology 119, 125
antinomies 136
Archaeology of Knowledge 94, 104, 164, 165
Arendt, H. 167
Aristarchian 57
Aristotelian 56, 58, 66
Atkinson, R.F. 156
Austin, J.L. 99
autographic 110
autonomous ix, 108, 112, 138
auxiliary hypothesis 19
Azande 124, 125, 168

Beck, L. W. 168
belief system 119, 126
Benjamin, W. 167
Birth of the Clinic 74, 78, 83, 162, 167
Bohm-Bawerk, E. von 151
Bouchard, D. 165
Bruno, G. 28
Buchdahl, G. 165
Buffon, G.L.L., Comte de 103
Burian, R. xii, 150
Butterfield, H. 155

Cairns, H. 164
Carnap, R. 32, 33, 37, 157
causation 28, 79, 162
classification 121, 123
closed predicament 124

cognitive scheme 124–125
Cohen, R. S. 152, 161
Collingwood, R.C. 155
commensurable 147
commodity 5
Conant, J. 33–36, 38, 81, 131, 157–159
conceptual schemes 32, 34, 35, 38, 42, 48,
    51, 81, 90, 97, 120, 123, 128, 129, 131,
    142, 168
conjectures 13, 18, 107, 114, 115, 152, 153,
    156
Conjectures and Refutations 13, 18, 152, 153,
    156
constant capital 15
constitutive xii, 139, 143
contested concepts 147
contradiction 15
convention 8, 37, 132, 137
conventional 66, 68, 72, 138, 142
Copernican system 56, 58, 59, 64–66, 71
Copernicus 40, 57, 160
culture 147
Currie, Gregory 160, 164, 166

D'Amico, R. 150, 154, 158
Darwin, C. 103, 104
Davidson, D. xiii, 126–131, 133, 135, 139,
    158, 168
Davis, K. S. 159
deconstruction xii
Descartes, R. 150
description 87, 102, 106
dialectic 165
Dilthey, W. 154, 155
discourse 78, 79, 104–106
discovery 8, 43, 48, 50, 151, 154
discursive formation 34, 103
Dolan, E. 164
doxa 97, 109
Drake, S. 158

Dreyfus, H. L. 162
dualism 107, 125, 129
Duhem, P. 42, 43, 51, 158, 159, 164

empiricism 9; constructive xii
Engels, F. 19, 43, 48–51, 159
Enlightenment 135
episteme 91, 93, 94, 97, 100
essentialism 11, 12, 25, 35, 114
Evans-Pritchard, E.E. 124, 168
evolution 104, 124, 142, 169
exegesis 87, 103
experimentation 69, 70, 168
explanation 6, 7, 12, 20, 55, 61, 87;
    institutional 6; structural 7

fallibilism xii
falsification 13, 17, 18, 38, 125
Farr, J. 166
Fekete, J. 150
Feyerabend, P. 38–42, 60, 71, 72, 158, 161
first world 109
Forte, A. ix, x, xi
Foucault, M. xiii, 73–86, 88–95, 97–107,
    119, 132, 145, 162–165, 167
framework xii, 32, 42, 81, 92, 116

Galileo, G. 39–41, 57, 65, 114–116, 158
Gallie, W.B. 147
Gaukroger, S. 158, 165
Geertz, C. 147
Gomperz, H. 151
Goodman, N. 110, 111, 117, 163, 167
Gordon, C. 166
Grayling, A.C. 131–135, 168, 169
Guerlac, H. 159

Habermas, J. 134, 136–143, 148, 169
Hacking, I. 38, 39, 68–71, 158, 161, 162
Hamilton, E. 164
Hanson, R.N. 159
Hegel, G.W.F. 1, 19, 129, 135, 136
Hegelian 1, 42, 60, 62, 66, 77, 95, 120, 165
Heidegger, M. 101, 165
Henahan, D. ix, x, 150
Herder, J.G. 154
hermeneutics 93, 111, 148, 156
heuristic 53, 56–58, 60, 65, 68, 71, 142
historical a priori 90; laws 22, 23, 27;
    reconstruction 84, 91, 93, 104, 106,
    115–117
historicism, two meanings of 20
history of ideas 84, 86, 98, 103, 106
Horton, R. 123–125, 168
Howson, C. 159
human essence 12
Human Understanding 62

Hume, D. 105, 131
Husserl, E. 158
hypothesis 19, 127, 131

ideal type 55
idealism 42, 120
Iggers, G. 150
incommensurability 129, 139
institutional analysis 3; logic 14
instrumentalism 11, 24, 25, 88, 89, 97, 137,
    141, 169
interpretation 21, 23, 25, 26, 28, 29, 36,
    40–42, 52, 61, 70, 92, 111, 112, 119, 122,
    127, 130, 140, 141, 144, 146, 147, 148

Johansson, I. 153

Kant, I. 32, 73, 90, 105, 131, 132, 134, 135,
    140, 149, 157, 167, 168
Kepler, J. 57, 115
King, L. J. 162
Koertge, N. 161
Krige, J. 166
Kuhn, T. 36, 44, 49, 58, 81, 131, 133,
    157–159, 161

Lakatos, I. 18, 52–73, 78, 107, 153, 160,
    161, 164
language xi, 139, 143
Laudan, L. xiii, 84, 86–89, 93, 163
Lavoisier, A. 43–51, 69, 159
law of supply and demand 7, 9
Lenin 19
Levi-Strauss, C. 121–123, 168
Logic of Scientific Discovery 8, 151, 154
Lysenko Affair 124
logicism xii

MacCarthy, T. 169
Mandelbaum, M. 154
Marcuse, H. 22, 138, 139, 154, 169
market 10
Marx, K. 2–9, 11–19, 24, 26, 43, 48–50, 135,
    136, 152, 153, 161
Marxism 74, 137
Maschler, C. 164
materialism 12
Meinecke, F. 155
Mellor, D.H. 165, 169
metaphor 76, 102
metaproblem 116
methodology 27, 36, 59, 60, 62, 67, 71, 105,
    123, 125, 160
modernism 85, 123
Mozart, W.A. 109, 110
Musgrave, A. 45, 159, 166

narrative 28, 55, 56, 59, 107, 108
Neurath, M. 152
Neurath, O. 152
Notturno, M. A. 151, 166
Nussbaum, M. 150

O'Hear, A. 156
Objective Knowledge 155, 157, 166, 167
objectivity xi, 24, 29, 108, 137, 138, 140, 148
observation 29, 36, 41, 43, 75, 77, 80, 82, 83, 85, 86, 101
open predicament 124
Open Society 2, 8, 13, 14, 22, 24, 26, 150, 151, 153, 156, 157, 166
Order of Things 74, 84, 94, 162–164
organic composition of capital 15

Papineau, D. 167
paradigm 34
perception 79, 97, 133
phenomenalism x, 41, 136
phlogiston 44–50, 159
Plato xii, 96, 97, 109, 129, 164
Platonic 113, 165
Polanyi, K. 156
Popper, K. xiii, 2–15, 17–31, 35, 38, 52, 58, 61–64, 67, 73, 87, 97, 105, 107, 108–114, 116, 117, 119, 123, 125, 131, 145, 146, 150–157, 160, 161, 165–167
positivism 11, 33, 37
Poverty of Historicism 2, 22, 23, 25, 26, 31, 150, 153, 155, 156
practice 97, 112, 137, 143
pragmatism xii, 136, 137
prediction 14, 19, 27, 166
prescription 87, 160
Priestly, J. 44, 46–50, 159
problem situation 21, 24, 107, 114, 117
problematic 34
pseudo-science 11, 67
psychoanalysis 13
psychologism 6, 111, 113
Ptolemaic system 56–59, 66
Ptolemy 160
purposive-rational 139
Putnam, H. xiii, 18, 30, 31, 35, 73–75, 107, 153, 157, 162

Quine, W.V.O. 37, 38, 119, 158, 160

Rabinow, P. 162
Rand, C. 22, 154, 155
Ranke, L. Von 119
rational reconstruction 20–22, 28, 30, 52, 59–61, 63, 64, 67, 68, 69–71, 73, 74, 81, 114, 115
rationality 30, 163

realism xi, 12, 24, 33, 41, 89, 118, 122
reference xi, 118, 119
refutation 8, 13, 14, 22, 27, 131
relativism x, 1, 23, 24, 30, 38, 42, 62, 68, 73, 76, 78, 89, 90, 92, 95, 97, 111, 117, 120, 122, 131, 142, 145
representation xi, 101, 119, 137, 143, 145
reproduction 110
research program 53–57, 59–61, 63–66, 71
research tradition 88
Ricardo, D. 4, 5, 151
Rickert, H. 155
Robinson, J. 151
Rodbertus, J. K. 49
Rosenberg, J. 120, 158, 168
rules 97, 101, 106

Sarkar, H. 160
Sartre, J.P. 122
scepticism xi, xii, 25, 30, 35, 38, 42, 75, 92, 95, 111, 117, 131, 134, 140, 143, 149, 169
Schilpp, P. A. 166
second world 109
semiology 165
Shapiro, J. J. 169
Sheridan Smith, A.M. 163, 164
situational analysis 23
situational logic 5, 16, 27
Skagestad, P. 166
Smith Bowen, E. 121, 125, 126
Socrates 96
sophistic x, 96, 120, 129
speech act 99
Sperber, D. 126, 127, 168
statement 98–102, 106, 164
strategies of reasoning 145
Strawson, P.F. 32, 132, 157, 168
Streissler, E. 155
Stroud, B. 168
style of reasoning 39, 42
Suchting, W.A. 154
surplus value 16, 48–50
symbolism 126, 127, 137, 141

Taruskin, R. ix, x, xi
teleology 90, 113
test 166
third world 34, 107–109, 111, 113, 117, 161, 167
Tilley, N. 155, 156
Toulmin, S. 62, 64, 95, 161
transcendental 90, 95, 105, 118, 131–133, 135, 138–143
translation 127–130
Troeltsch, E. 154
truth 82, 129, 148, 163

understanding 62, 114, 137–139, 141, 142
Unended Quest 150, 151, 155

value, labor theory of 3–5, 7–12, 14–16, 24, 26
variable capital 15
verification 63, 135
Vico, G. 154
Vienna Circle 13

Wartofsky, M. 161
Weber, M. 155
Weeks, J. 10, 152
Windelband, W. 155
Wittgenstein, L. 62, 161
Wolfson, M 151
work 139
Worral, J. 160, 164